2

INTERNATIONAL PSYCHIATRY CLINICS

APPLICATION TO MAIL AT SECOND CLASS POSTAGE RATE PENDING AT BOSTON, MASSACHU-
SETTS. PUBLISHED QUARTERLY BY LITTLE, BROWN AND COMPANY, 34 BEACON STREET,
BOSTON, MASSACHUSETTS.

SUBSCRIPTION RATE $18.50 PER YEAR. FOREIGN RATE $21.00 PER YEAR.

FORENSIC PSYCHIATRY
AND CHILD PSYCHIATRY

EDITED BY

D. Ewen Cameron, M.D.

Albany Medical College
Veterans Administration Hospital
Albany, N.Y.

BOSTON
LITTLE, BROWN AND COMPANY
© 1965 BY LITTLE, BROWN AND COMPANY (INC.)

INTERNATIONAL PSYCHIATRY CLINICS

JANUARY 1965

VOL. 2 . NO. 1

Contributors

D. EWEN CAMERON, M.D., Editor
Research Professor, Albany Medical College
Director, Psychiatry and Aging Research Laboratories,
Veterans Administration Hospital, Albany, New York
Formerly Chairman, Department of Psychiatry, Allan Memorial Institute,
McGill University, Montreal

RAYMOND BOYER, Ph.D.
Research Associate, McGill University Clinic in Forensic Psychiatry,
Montreal

BRUNO M. CORMIER, M.D.
Assistant Professor, McGill University, Montreal
Director, Forensic Clinic, Allan Memorial Institute, Montreal
Associate Psychiatrist, Royal Victoria Hospital, Montreal

FRED J. DILL, B.Sc.
Department of Pediatrics, University of British Columbia, Vancouver

CLARENCE B. FARRAR, M.D.
Editor, American Journal of Psychiatry, Toronto

KENNETH G. GRAY, Q.C., M.D.
Professor of Forensic Psychiatry, Department of Psychiatry, University
of Toronto, Toronto

ROBERT O. JONES, M.D.
Professor of Psychiatry, Dalhousie University, Halifax

MIRIAM KENNEDY, P.S.W.
Social Worker, Department of Psychiatry, McGill University, Montreal
Research Associate, McGill University Clinic in Forensic Psychiatry,
Montreal

v

DENIS LAZURE, M.D.

Director, Child Psychiatry Department, Hôpital Ste-Justine, Montreal
Associate Professor in Psychiatry, University of Montreal Medical School,
Montreal
Associate Director, Psychiatric Services, Quebec Provincial Department
of Health

NOËL MAILLOUX, Ph.D.

Professor, Institut de Psychologie, University of Montreal, Montreal
Director, Centre de Recherches en Relations Humaines, Montreal

JAMES R. MILLER, Ph.D.

Department of Pediatrics, University of British Columbia, Vancouver

ANTON OBERT, P.S.W.

Social Worker, Department of Psychiatry, McGill University, Montreal
Research Associate, McGill University Clinic in Forensic Psychiatry,
Montreal

M. SAM RABINOVITCH, Ph.D.

Department of Psychology, Montreal Children's Hospital, Montreal
and McGill University, Montreal

EDWARD J. ROSEN, M.D.

Assistant Professor, Department of Psychiatry, Faculty of Medicine,
University of Toronto, Toronto
Director, Child and Adolescent Unit, Toronto Psychiatric Hospital,
Toronto

JADWIGA M. SANGOWICZ, M.D.

Lecturer in Psychiatry, McGill University, Montreal
Assistant Psychiatrist, Royal Victoria Hospital, Montreal
Psychiatrist in McGill University Clinic in Forensic Psychiatry, Montreal

ANDRÉ L. THIFFAULT

Psychologist, Department of Psychiatry, McGill University, Montreal
Research Associate, McGill University Clinic in Forensic Psychiatry,
Montreal

Preface

This Canadian volume of the *International Psychiatry Clinics* presents work done in two fields of major interest in Canadian psychiatry: forensic psychiatry and child psychiatry. In Canada these two fields have attracted men of exceptional capacity. Their contributions well exemplify the vigor and vitality with which psychiatry is developing, not only in these fields but in general in this country.

D. EWEN CAMERON

Contents

Forensic Psychiatry

Child Psychiatry

FORENSIC PSYCHIATRY

Criminal Process and
Emotional Growth

BRUNO M. CORMIER, MIRIAM KENNEDY,
JADWIGA M. SANGOWICZ, RAYMOND
BOYER, ANDRÉ L. THIFFAULT, AND
ANTON OBERT

Habitual criminality commonly implies a state of almost continuous criminal activity. It conveys the idea of an irreversible antisocial course of behavior, affecting the whole life-span, in which the total personality is involved. Nevertheless, when we look at the evidence for the irreversibility of habitual criminality, we do not find much to confirm such a belief. Both statistical surveys and clinical studies point to the fact that the persistent criminal is capable of changing with time. There is not yet, however, a comprehensive account of the changes that take place within a criminal life. While the natural history of the major mental illnesses has been precisely described by the classic psychiatrists, the natural history of criminal behavior largely remains to be written. In this paper we will attempt the study of the criminal process as it evolved in an individual criminal career. We will follow and interpret the development by means of psychiatric concepts and draw inferences arising from our material.

The authors dedicate this paper to Sheldon and Eleanor Glueck, for their contribution to the science of delinquent behavior.
This paper is part of a research program financed by Dominion-Provincial Mental Health Grant 604–5–108, and carried out in the Department of Psychiatry, McGill University.

CRIMINAL PROCESS

The term "process" is employed here in the same sense as in medicine, to designate the onset, evolution, and outcome of a physical or psychiatric disease. "Process" is a dynamic term involving movement, passage, phase, variation, transformation, regression, progression, remission, and exacerbation. A process takes place in time, and may be of short or long duration. Its evolution may be slow or rapid. A process may vary in severity, be reversible or irreversible, benign or malignant, and normal or pathological.

The evolution of a pathological process can be taken as synonymous for what clinicians call the "natural history" of a disease, on which they used to place great emphasis. Once a disease was diagnosed, the symptoms and the minutiae observed in its development were all-important. They were the means of foreseeing favorable changes or a fatal issue for clinicians who had few therapeutic procedures to interfere with the natural evolution of the process. The detection of the organic, anatomo-pathological, and physiological changes that are reflected in the symptoms; the uncovering of causes; and ultimately the discovery of symptomatic or specific therapeutics placed the modern clinician in a new role. Many diseases no longer follow their natural history. By treatment, they are arrested or their course is modified.

Like medical clinicians, the psychiatrists of the past, with few therapeutic means at their disposal, were largely observers of the natural history of mental illnesses. These took their various courses, such as spontaneous cure and remission, sporadic recurrence, or deterioration. In more recent times, psychiatrists began to intervene in mental pathological processes. Mental illnesses can be arrested, cured, or the evolution changed.

A parallel can be drawn between disease process and pathological behavior process. The latter, too, has a natural history which, like its counterparts in medicine and psychiatry, can be transient, repetitive, episodic, benign or severe, incidental or chronic. We will here confine ourselves to a specific type of criminal process, referred to in an earlier study as "primary delinquency," which, because of its severity, duration, and infringement on human rights and society, should rightly be considered as a very serious social disorder.

Primary delinquency is a pathological process, characterized by a failure of socialization, manifesting itself as early as latency, a failure which is conducive to persistent delinquency in youth and to habitual criminality in later life. Primary delinquency is seen as a continuum, starting early in life, undergoing many transformations in adolescence and maturity. Thus the antisocial acting out of the primary delinquent is not divided into a period of juvenile delinquency and adult criminality according to chronological age. The criminality of the primary delinquent must be seen as an evolution of his early delinquency which now takes new shapes and forms. Antisocial behavior for him is not merely a succession of offenses, but the unfolding and development of a process that takes place in time and space and is accompanied by many psychological changes (7, 8).

STATISTICAL STUDIES ON THE ABATEMENT OF CRIMINALITY WITH AGE

Investigations, some carried out over a century ago, indicate that habitual criminality reaches a peak and is followed by a steady decline. As early as 1833, Quêtelet, who may be considered the father of criminal statistics, was one of the first to make a scientific and detailed survey. Among his many important findings, some of the most interesting to us are the ones related to criminality and age. Quêtelet observed that the incidence of criminality attained a maximum at age 25, and from then on there was a steady decline. As Quêtelet's books are not available to us, we quote from Sellin and the Gluecks, who refer to the original material. Quêtelet held that, "Among all the causes that influence the growth and abatement of the penchant for crime, age is without question the most energetic." He also believed that the inclination towards crime "attains the maximum at about the age of 25 when physical development has almost been completed; . . . the intellectual and the moral growth, which is slower, later abates the penchant for crime, which diminishes still later due to the enfeeblement of physical vitality and the passions" (20, 21).

Quêtelet's organic explanation may be subject to discussion, but the facts he established in 1833 are still valid and are confirmed by contemporary statistics. Thorsten Sellin makes mention of a number of European statistical studies which bear out Quêtelet's original assumption. A significant finding is that, "The younger a person is when he is first convicted of a crime, the greater is the likelihood that he will be convicted again and that he will continue to commit crimes over a longer period" (25).

We have examined Canadian federal penal statistics from 1935 to the present, and have discovered the same trend. In the ages between 20 and 30, there is a peak in the number of inmates admitted to penitentiary, and from then on a steady and continuous decline. There are half as many penitentiary admissions of men between ages 30 and 40 as there are of men between ages 20 and 30, and half as many again after age 40. When the age groups of the Quebec penitentiary population for 1960 are compared with the corresponding age groups in the male population of the Province of Quebec, we find the following: the group of young offenders in the early twenties form 20.9 percent of the penitentiary population, while this same group in society as a whole is 10.8 percent. The group of offenders in the forties, on the contrary, are 17.9 percent of the penitentiary population while the same group outside are 33.8 percent. There is an almost complete reversal of statistics which cannot be explained by the death rate of the criminal or the general population, but must be interpreted as an indication that recidivists as they grow older stay out of the penitentiary (3, 6).

THE SCIENCE OF HUMAN BEHAVIOR
AND THE CRIMINAL PROCESS

A major contribution in the field of delinquency is the contemporary work of Sheldon and Eleanor Glueck. Their aim was primarily to build a prediction scale for delinquent behavior and this aspect has been much discussed. Looking at their work in its totality, it may well be that their chief contribution goes beyond the field of prediction. They have added to our knowledge perhaps most significantly by broadening the whole area of clinical criminology which, following the first impact of psychonanalytic theory, was too exclusively preoccupied with the psychogenesis of the criminal act rather than the exploration of the total life. Since the work of the Gluecks, and other longitudinal studies by people like Shaw (26), and Healy and Bronner (15), it is as important to know the total life of the individual offender as it is the many offenses which are part of that life. Such studies have opened the way to a dynamic interpretation of the natural history of criminality.

The Gluecks have given us a multifactorial analysis combining a statistical, sociological, and clinical approach. What makes this study unique is that it is based on two large samples, one taken over a 10-year period, and the other analyzed and reanalyzed over 15 years. In *Juvenile Delinquents Grow Up*, the authors report on 1,000 offenders who were observed over a period of 15 years. After 5 years of observation, it was noted that 14.6 percent of the entire group could be classified as nonoffenders. In the second follow-up, this number had risen to 26.8 percent, and by the third follow-up, the number had increased to 36.6 percent. At the 15-year follow-up, the average age of these offenders was 29.54. The Gluecks are now in the process of analyzing this group 20 years after. It will be interesting to learn if this trend of lessening criminality with age is continued.

The Gluecks, after studying many criminal careers over many years, conclude that "aging is the only factor that emerges as significant in the reformative process when our cases are analyzed en masse." They also observed that among the men "who remain criminalistic throughout these years of observation there was a notable and on the whole a favorable change in the character of their offense" (11, 12, 13).

CLINICAL STUDIES OF
THE CRIMINAL PROCESS

To date there have been few systematic, psychiatric or psychoanalytic attempts to determine what psychological changes accompany the evolution of criminality and its abatement. There is outstanding work, particularly in the etiology of juvenile delinquency where the roots of the delinquent process have been traced in detail. The end product, the habitual, has been well described by clinicians who work in this field, but a link in continuity is lacking. It is difficult to follow a criminal career in its duration, to get a picture of the process as a whole. Workers dealing with young offenders lose their contact with them after adolescence, and those who see and study habitual criminals seldom have the opportunity to know them when they were juvenile delinquents. Their investigation is necessarily retrospective.

With regard to the literature on juvenile delinquency, we have a mass of material since the early work of Aichhorn (1), who first applied psychoanalytic concepts to the treatment of delinquent adolescents. Since then there has been a close investigation of the character formation of the antisocial child and we are particularly indebted to such clinicians as Friedlander and Johnson (10, 16). Bettelheim, Redl and Wineman, and Mailloux (4, 22, 18) have investigated further the treatment of young delinquents in specially designed reeducative schools, providing us with full studies of such children in groups. In observing the delinquent child individually, as well as his interaction with others, such persons have greatly enlarged our knowledge of the process of pathological socialization.

There are also many excellent, well-documented studies on individual adult offenders; in particular, the work of Karpman (17), who pioneered such investigation in America and published complete case studies. Despite the value of his material, Karpman failed to provide a workable concept which would enable us to speak in psychiatric terms of the evolution and termination of a criminal course.

Schmideberg, who has had great experience in the treatment of criminals, has provided most useful comments about the maturation and integration of the superego. In her view, the superego as well as the ego continues to mature throughout life, creating possibilities for an increasing capacity for identification and sublimation, and a more harmonious integration of the personality. The personality structure of so-called hardened criminals is not as rigidly fixed as was previously believed, and even after reaching maturity there are natural possibilities for emotional growth (24).

The McGill research group has explored the phenomenon of criminality in individuals in its changing aspects and transformations. The following hypothesis was developed in a paper on the subject of abatement of criminality: the individual suffering from a behavior disorder generally makes use of alloplastic solutions, acting out a conflict rather than living it inwardly. The alloplastic symptom formation which is not basically ego-disruptive, does not, therefore, alter the capacity for a correct perception of reality, and there remains the possibility of a progression toward more mature formations. The delinquency of latency and puberty tends to be of a diffuse, free-floating quality, but by early adulthood there is the beginning of specialization, and though the individual may become more aggressive, he is also more selective and purposeful. This is already the first beginnings of abatement to the extent that the offender begin to accept some social norms aside from his criminal practice. With the passing of the years, the repetitive criminal act does not bring the anticipated gratification. Whether in the late twenties, the thirties, or the forties, he begins for the first time to feel anxiety and depression, which were previously present but were repressed or discharged by alloplastic mechanisms.

He becomes painfully aware of such autoplastic symptom formations as the alloplastic mechanisms break down. This stage, which we call the saturation point, is often accompanied by severe symptomatology but is, nevertheless, in terms of the total personality a progression, a late continuation of a maturation process arrested at an earlier level. As emotional suffering is now felt, there is a motivation for change which takes place with or without outside assistance (8). Age is in itself not the cause of the abatement of criminality, but is seen as a time dimension which includes "lived time" (*temps vécu*, so well described by Minkowsky) and the time still to be lived; and, in between, the fleeting, ungraspable, present moment (19).

EMOTIONAL GROWTH AND
THE PROCESS OF SOCIALIZATION

Immaturity, a term widely employed, is a vague, imprecisely defined concept, pathognomonic of no specific diagnosis or nosological entity. Generally, it designates an individual, adult in years but infantile in his feelings, attitudes, and behavior. Immaturity infers some defect in normal emotional development, a lack of acquired control over infantile modes of reaction in the early formative years which may in some children become evident as early as latency in persistent delinquency taking the final form of an adult criminality. To understand this pathological outcome, let us review the early emotional development, the feelings a child must work through in order to achieve maturity. Analysis of adults, direct observation of infants, and later the analysis of children have enabled the reconstruction of early feelings and responses of the infant and growing child. They can be briefly summarized:

1. The primary feeling that one is the world, with the ensuing inability to differentiate what is the ego, and what is the nonego.
2. The split of the external and internal world into good and bad objects, according to narcissistic feelings of gratification or frustration.
3. The primacy of the pleasure principle and the belief that the world is for one's egotistical satisfaction.
4. The urgent need for immediate discharge.
5. The difficulty to perceive ambivalent feelings, and later to integrate and accept ambivalent feelings toward an object.
6. The frequent passage from a state of bliss to a state of rage.
7. The belief in one's omnipotence.

These feelings and responses are all vividly experienced by the infant and growing child, at first barely protected from his instincts, in time progressively tamed by the emergence and recognition of controls from within and without, and the discovery of his own identity and that of others. The weak barriers and controls of the ill-defined identity of the infant are called "archaic ego" and "archaic superego." From this archaic ego and superego ultimately emerge the ego with its mechanisms of defense, and the superego with its condemnation and condonation. After many oscillations, regressions, and progressions into the oral, anal, and genital stages, and ultimately with the gradual resolution of the oedipal situation, a child is sufficiently socialized to move outside his own family, to go to school, and to widen his contacts. By the end of adolescence, social values and responsibilities are incorporated and consolidated, the individual has become a personally and socially responsible member of society, able to care for himself and others and to obey a social code.

An infant born asocial, at the mercy of his instincts, has to learn to give up many early forms of behavior, to repress many primitive emotions in the process of maturation. The child depends upon important figures in the family constellation to help him to achieve this end and to grow normally. If there is interference in this process, normal growth is replaced by symptom formations or character disorder, or both.

MATURITY, IMMATURITY, AND LATE MATURATION

We have said that immaturity is ill-defined, and there is good and sufficient reason why the concept is difficult to grasp, quantify, and qualify. Most authors are in agreement in one respect: emotional growth is not a gradual, even process. In the healthiest, best integrated development there are latent periods, spurts, interlocking and interrelated cycles. Maturity may be compared to a field where fertile ground exists side by side with arid areas and patches of spotty, unequal growth. Practically speaking, immaturity—the total absence of maturity—is incompatible with life. An irreducible minimum is essential if only to maintain existence. On the other hand, it is hardly possible to define the limit of maturity a man can achieve. Between these two opposite points, maturity and immaturity, there is every degree of quality.

A useful concept in studying this phenomenon is that of late maturation, defined here as the acquisition late in life of barriers and controls, and of the gradual gaining of a true image of oneself and others, with the resulting capacity to relate to the world. These qualities are normally acquired in the early formative years and during adolescence. If we are to reach an understanding of the abatement of persistent criminality through the path of late maturation, we are immediately confronted with the complex problem of attempting to quantify and qualify the degree of maturity within an individual criminal career, not once but over and over again in the life continuum. Sullivan, Grant, and Grant (27) describe the psychological development of interpersonal maturity in terms of successive levels of integration. A crucial interpersonal problem is defined for each level, which must be solved before further progress can occur. These problems encompass the intricate development of object relationships encountered by a child passing through the oral, anal, and oedipal phases described in psychoanalytic theory. From this theoretical framework, Grant and Grant (14) devised an interpersonal maturity scale and formed therapeutic groups for nonconformist subjects in the Navy who fell into the various defined levels of integration. The aim was to assess how these groups responded to therapeutic techniques. In Canada, Russon (23), whose work is based on Sullivan and the Grants, proposed a classification for offenders; and Talhurst (28) has been applying this classification for the assessment and treatment of inmates in the Prince Albert, Saskatchewan, penitentiary.

Our view on the subject of maturity, immaturity, and late maturity as it relates to the process of socialization and delinquency has been somewhat different. Though not divorced from theoretical consideration, our classification is based primarily on a psychiatric assessment of the offender with special regard to the age at which he becomes involved in incidental or habitual delinquency and the quality and extent of the involvement. From these two sets of clinical data we have grouped the offender in three major categories: primary, secondary, and late delinquent, according to the age at which he becomes involved in delinquency. We have assumed certain levels of integration of maturity and immaturity, but have not defined them as sharply as Sullivan and the Grants. We have delineated retrospectively the changes taking place in a delinquent life from its onset in childhood to the time when we first meet an adult criminal. Then we analyze further observed changes as they occur. The clinical frame of reference we use to evaluate these changes is described later. It by no means contradicts the concepts of Sullivan and the Grants. Both are conducive to treatment and to the evaluation of treatment.

CLINICAL STUDY

In the case history we are presenting it is possible to follow the psychogensis of the criminal career as it unfolds. Our aim, however, in writing the life of Jacques B. is rather to describe the opposite, the decline of criminality. It is the psychogenesis of a reverse process, the undoing of a criminal life, an evolution no less complex. Just as frustrating to the offender and to society as the leading of a criminal life is the painful road that the offender must follow before finding, among the law abiding, those that he will accept, and who will not reject him. This new rapport is possible as the deliquent learns to come to terms with the demands of society, and society in turn no longer repudiates him.

We will outline the history of Jacques B.; trace the evolution of his delinquency through latency, adolescence, and maturity; and show how, as his delinquency changes in quality and severity, these transformations were accompanied by and were the reflection of changes in his total personality.

CASE HISTORY

Jacques B. is a young French Canadian, born in 1931 in a small town in Quebec. His parents, now in their fifties, separated in 1942. Jacques is the first son and third child of a family of five; he is followed by one brother who is three years younger, and a sister. The father is a laborer, intelligent but with scanty education; the mother's background is socially higher. The drive for achievement comes from the mother, and in spite of economic reverses and other stresses, the siblings have done well. One sister is married, one is a teacher, and the third a secretary; the brother is a skilled worker.

The father was a poor provider and somewhat given to drink. The marriage was an unhappy one. The mother had high standards and was unwilling to make compromises. Jacques was born during the depression of the 1930's when the father was chronically out of work and the mother forced to depend upon the charity of her more fortunate family.

Jacques, a premature baby, was sickly and hard to rear. He had feeding difficulties, and in the first few years of his life suffered from rickets and almost every childhood disease. He remained undersized until puberty. He was, moreover, an exceptionally active child, restless and subject to temper tantrums. Behavioral difficulties could in part be traced to the inconsistency of his unbringing, but we do not know exactly why the mother had such exceptional trouble with this child from the start. She was able to handle her other children well. It was as if she did not have enough to give this sickly but overactive child who demanded so much more than the others. The father was an easy-going man when things went well, with a temper when crossed. He was pleased that his first-born son resembled him and boasted about his "toughness," favoring and spoiling him, but he lost his temper rapidly when Jacques displeased him. He would then shout at the child and beat him. Jacques reacted to attempts at discipline by screaming and temper tantrums.

In later childhood, his physical condition improved and his motor development was normal, but he did not overcome his early infantile patterns. When he was opposed he responded with rage; when things went his way, he showed a very sunny, winning disposition. He could not come to terms with adults who sometimes punished, but mostly gave in to him.

By age six, Jacques was such a behavior problem that he could not be accepted in an ordinary school and he was sent to a boarding school. Though there was no intellectual deficit, he was unteachable. With his behavioral difficulties and emotional disturbance, the school soon refused to keep him. Therefore, he was removed to a mental hospital in a group setting for retarded and disturbed children. He remained there for about seven months and remembers this episode as a very punishing one as he was severely disciplined.

Being neither retarded nor psychotic, he was returned home and there followed in the next three years placment in at least two more boarding schools.

In latency, as early as age six, a pattern of stealing developed. At first Jacques stole only from his mother, but he soon extended his activities and began to steal outside the home. He did not involve his younger brother or look for partners but he stole alone. As this delinquency could not be stopped, he was sent to a reform school at the age of nine. This was for him at the time another in a series of institutional placements. He spent about eighteen months there, where he was a severe disciplinary problem and was frequently punished. When he returned home at age 11, he was as uncontrollable as before and was quickly placed in another boarding school, where again he remained only briefly.

In 1942 at age 11, there was an important change in the family which greatly affected Jacques. The father joined the Army, and in consequence found himself away from home, with a steady source of income and some independence. He shed the responsibilities of his disappointing marriage and became involved in an affair which developed into a permanent union. His wife found herself abandoned, and from then on she had to fend for herself and be the guardian of the family.

Jacques was home when the father deserted, and his feeling against him was one of anger and a sense of betrayal. Fifteen years later, he could say, in defending his way of life, "What is a bad man is my father—not me." He wished to help his mother and felt protective, but he would no more accept her control than previously. On the contrary, he believed that he should now be the man in the family and he suffered intense rejection when she was forced to place him, like the other children. This resulted in increased delinquent activity, with a return to reform school, where he remained for the next 3½ years, until he was 15.

During this placement, Jacques took great pride in his achievement as an outstandingly bad boy. He often ran away, not so much because he had any specific place to run to, or out of great dislike of the school, but from restlessness and bravado. For this and other misbehavior he received considerable corporal punishment and he boasted that he had the strap 36 times in one year—in his mind a record. He became a kind of champion of the group of bad boys and claimed that he could accept severe punishment without shedding a tear. This apparent callousness was only a facade, for along with his struggle against authority, a new influence was felt.

For the first time in his life, Jacques experienced and accepted other people's ambivalence toward him which involved both punishment and reward. A teacher was able to establish a relationship. This man, unlike the others, could make Jacques cry when he punished him because he was sorry, but he was also very kind to him and he could, as Jacques said, "make me dream." He told him stories and described the wonders of life. For the first time, Jacques became interested in matters outside his immediate environment and was able at last to learn. This good experience was either too brief or did not go far enough to make a change in his pattern at the time. Along with his real love toward the teacher, the running away and the stealing continued, bringing him into frequent contact with the juvenile court.

His pattern followed what might be called the "normal course" of adolescent delinquency. It was also at the service of his need to establish dominion over his parents and, through them, other male and female figures, the whole adult world. He created situations where he tested adults to the point where they were forced to reject and punish him. As a result, he retaliated and then tried to exploit further. For example, a woman probation officer with a reputation for strictness nevertheless interceded for him in his numerous escapades. Once, while waiting with her at the juvenile court, Jacques picked a man's pocket and stole his wallet. In spite of his affection for Miss S., he could not avoid this display of expertise and the compulsion to see how far he could go and still be able to secure her help and interest.

Another time, when Jacques was 13 and his mother was working in an institution, he was permitted to live with her. He seemed very happy in this arrangement, where he had the mother almost exclusively to himself, but he could not tolerate the situation and almost immediately stole some money. The mother was forced to part with him.

As well as his need to be totally accepted was his quite conscious wish to control his family. He regarded himself as the oldest son, the head of the home, and as such he had the right to give orders. He wanted to supplant the father, but to be very generous and giving, though imposing his goodness aggressively.

Jacques' relationship with men followed much the same pattern of testing, exploitation, and retaliation. At 15 his father was reached by the court, and he offered to take the boy to live with him. Unrealistically, Jacques expected much from this reunion, but the father apparently took little interest and allowed the boy to drift. Moreover, when a roomer in the same house took advantage of him homosexually and this was reported to the father, the latter, according to Jacques, did not protect him but instead blackmailed the man and demanded money. He left his father's home and became a young vagrant, living as a homosexual, and when he grew a little older, as a male prostitute and thief. His sexual practice, which soon also included heterosexuality, was depersonalized at the time, divorced from any emotional content, though in his contacts with women he began to derive increasing physical satisfaction.

Toward the end of his adolescence, Jacques presented a picture of a young man poorly controlled, living off homosexuality and theft, wandering and footloose. His stealing was disorganized, almost spontaneous, in the same way that his wanderings were impulsive rather than with a fixed objective and a plan in mind.

About this time Jacques first became interested in work. This was sporadic but seemed to satisfy a real need, in accord perhaps with his overflowing physical vitality. There were bouts of compulsive work, mostly in the woods as a lumberjack. He also began to make distinctions and to find a difference between the sexual pleasure he obtained for his own satisfaction and that of gaining a living or exploiting others. By age 18, he had grown into a very hardy, physically agile young man, good looking, who took pride in his strength, his sexual capacity, and his ability to work very hard when he wished.

From then on delinquency lost its diffuse, adolescent quality and became organized. He gradually gave up homosexuality as a means of making money, in favor of pimping. The exploitation of women thus became a commercial venture rather than adolescent acting out. A change took place in his criminal pattern. It became specialized and he resorted more and more to unarmed break, entry, and theft. He outgrew his habit of aimless wandering. This specialization, however, brought him into increasingly sharp conflict with the law.

Until Jacques was 22, he succeeded in keeping out of very serious trouble, and served only small sentences. He gave up some of his adolescent brashness after an encounter with a judge where he was given a 10-month sentence, largely for insolence. He became in effect a young criminal with the inevitable consequences of frequent arrest and lengthening sentences. By age 23 he was well integrated in criminal society, with many years to go before there would be any change in his pattern. Though living largely by theft, he had not relinquished contact with prostitutes, either commercially or personally.

During most of Jacques' adolescence he had been at odds with his family, but after age 20 there was a conscious wish to be restored, though on his own terms, not as a repentant black sheep but as the first son, the leader. The family did not discard him and the mother actively helped him when she could. Nevertheless, his ambivalent feelings made reconciliation difficult.

A change in Jacques' life occurred when he was 23. He met a girl, Marie F., some two years younger than himself, with whom he initiated what appeared to be a casual affair. The girl was a foundling, adopted by a family with whom she lived in her childhood. When her adoptive parents died, she was placed in an orphanage until age 17. Jacques soon started Marie into a career of prostitution. She was quickly picked up by the police and spent a few days in jail. Thereupon she gave up this life, which she did not like, and Jacques agreed, as he found himself attached. He felt a kinship for this girl who had no family and had, like him, spent years of her girlhood in institutions and had then to face the world alone. The relationship deepened, and when he was arrested on a charge of theft at age 24 and sentenced to two years in penitentiary, she promised to wait for him. He did not take this seriously, having never thought of being faithful to anyone himself nor believing that a woman would be faithful to him. The two-year sentence, of which he served some 19 months, passed easily enough and he returned to society when he was 25. To his real surprise, he found that Marie had kept her promise, waited for him, looked after his belongings, worked, and saved money. He was greatly moved because she had done so much without making any demands, and they married shortly after his release.

From then on, a different life began for Jacques B. For the first time he had the experience of making a home with someone and it was gratifying. He took a job and he discovered satisfaction in what he called being a real family man. To him this meant acquiring expensive furniture on credit and owning a car. He fell increasingly into debt because he could not bear to wait for anything he wanted.

He was now anxious to reestablish himself with his own family. They had some reservations about his marriage and Jacques was annoyed at this and determined to overcome their objections. He felt that he could prove his success as a husband by the display of a fine home and by giving them expensive gifts. Here again he displayed his pattern of domination through a combination of aggression and seduction. His attempts left him unsatisfied as he felt that his family did not think of him and his wife as equal, and that he was still excluded.

The marriage, however, was a happy one, though the debts troubled him. After ten months he grew restless; he met some of his previous criminal friends and they induced him rather easily to become a partner. What is remarkable here is not so much that he was tempted to return to stealing, but that for almost a year he had worked at the one job and, even more important, that his object in stealing had now changed. He wanted to maintain the life he found increasingly good. He stole to protect his investment. However, instead of paying debts, he spent the money irrationally, as before. This upset him but he could no longer stop. Angry with himself, and unhappy, he took more risks, with the result that he was picked up again and faced a number of charges of break, entry, and theft. This time the sentence was longer: two years and three months. The home which he so prized had to be given up, the furniture was repossessed. He lost his car, and his wife was forced again to live a life of poverty. He faced this prison sentence with anxiety, and greatly lessened self-esteem and confidence. For the first time in his life, he suffered real heartache about another person, his wife. It was some months after these events, while serving his sentence, that he was interviewed by us.

Jacques had requested help from the professional staff in the penitentiary and was eventually referred as a research subject. His object was to seek advice about his marriage, and his symptoms of growing tension and anxiety. This was significant, as he had never previously felt he needed help in serving a sentence or worried about his life outside. He was now in a state of great resentment against his wife and family, mingled with real concern. He was afraid he would lose his wife and he wanted his family to act for him and to take care of her. Neither wife nor family hastened to obey his commands, and he felt intensely frustrated as a result. To make matters worse, his wife became ill, lost her job, was destitute, and took to prostitution again, though very briefly. Jacques could forgive this, as prostitution to him was still a way to earn a living. He could not tolerate her refusal to accept his family, or the fact that she was reputed to be unfaithful with a friend of his. This story reached him in prison and made him furious. He found himself overcome with anger, yet the realization came ever more keenly how much he loved his wife, in spite of what seemed to him her capricious as well as bad behavior.

The wife was a level-headed and intelligent young woman, who was thrown by circumstances into an irregular life but looked for security. Moreover, though angry with Jacques and bitter at his dereliction, she loved him. She was willing to overlook the past and admitted freely her own fall from grace. She therefore agreed to take the first step to establish contact with his family. This turned out well, and they grew fond of her. She ended by living with them and found steady work.

During this crisis in the relationship, Jacques' depression deepened. From blaming others—his mother for not loving him enough, his father for deserting him, his wife for misconduct—he began to blame himself. This alternated with bouts of rage against his wife and a feeling of being abandoned. He developed suicidal ruminations, though there was not a suicide attempt.

The turning point occurred in an interview some three months after contact with the research group. He was in a mood of intense anger and jealousy against his wife, accusing her of infidelity and saying that he was finished with her. From then he suddenly veered to extreme self-blame, saying that Marie had been a good girl when he first met her, and it was he who had debauched her. He opened out in an emotionally-charged, almost uncontrollable description of his life in the past, and recounted what he himself described to be the worst and most sordid aspects of his life as a male prostitute, a homosexual, and a practicer of all kinds of sexual perversion for gain and also for the pleasure he enjoyed in exploiting his physical prowess and his hold over people. Though apparently exposing his own transgression throughout this exhibition, his account was at the same time an attack, an act of aggression against the interviewer, and a testing out of her response. He was exhausted when he finished his recital and ended by acknowledging that for the first time he suffered through love; love for another included anxiety, jealousy, and anger. He accepted the ambivalent feelings in the relationship, and the fact that he was no longer free. He must give up some liberty if he wished to maintain his marriage. Almost with chagrin, he admitted that his wife could hurt him badly and that he still wanted her.

From then on there was a change in his attitude within the prison as well as toward his wife and family. He showed a growing capacity to accept discipline and he no longer lost his temper so frequently. He was among the first to be sent to a new prerelease camp and he began to plan for his future. He was a very confident man when he was released. He found work quickly and furnished a pleasant home without getting into debt.

As well as reestablishing contact with his mother and siblings, he turned again to his father and found that life had changed him too. He forgave his father, and they became friendly. Jacques is the only family member who is in touch with the father; the mother and the other children have disowned him. It seems that these two most aggressive and difficult personalities understand one another.

Jacques' career as an honest man, though checkered, has been marked by a determined struggle to maintain himself. A first crisis came with a loss of his job, due to general unemployment, just as his child, a son, was born. He tried to find work but he experienced a a real temptation to steal, which he overcame. He accepted instead, for the first time, the minimum standards of unemployment insurance until he found a job.

Periods of unemployment continued, as his work, though well paid, was seasonal. When employed he was overconfident and contracted debts, not out of line with his income while working, but a source of trouble when he had to live on unemployment insurance. Two and a half years after his release, his difficulties accumulated as by then he had a second child, born prematurely, and had suffered a work accident which laid him off for some time. He began to look for something more permanent than seasonal work and put a great deal of energy into his plans. When they failed, he grew correspondingly dissappointed and at the same time more reluctant to subsist on meager unemplyoment insurance. In this situation, a return to his former pattern, a prospect which both attracted and repelled him, was almost inevitable. He found himself drifting toward his old associates, half against his will, but with a compulsion to return. As he said, "After all, I have been stealing since I was five and six years old." During this period of a few weeks he was unstable, restless, and at odds with his wife, who was adamant that she would leave him if he became criminal but who continued to provide comfort and help. He would not keep appointments to see us, though he did not absolutely break the contact. During this crisis, we were mainly supportive of the wife and helped her contain the situation.

At first Jacques contented himself with advising his friends how to plan burglaries; then he went along once as a partner, but the attempt failed. This seemed to give him both satisfaction and great annoyance. Eventually, he committed one successful break and entry by himself. He gave his wife all the proceeds (enough to pay the outstanding debts), and kept nothing for himself. This was followed by an immediate reduction of tension and a revulsion from his criminal associates. He threw away his burglar tools. He felt that he had been ill and was now well again. He was intensely grateful to his wife for standing by him and yet refusing to countenance his backsliding. In contrast to his previous pattern, he did not continue stealing until he was caught, but stopped at once and began to look very purposefully for a way out. All his forces now seemed redirected.

This single relapse into criminality took place some two years ago. There has been a continuing contact with this clinic. Jacques has had his periods of dissatisfaction and restlessness but has given no indication to his wife or ourselves of a compulsion to return to criminality. His friends and associates are now among the law-abiding.

Despite Jacques B.'s dangerous temporary return to criminality, his chances appear better now for a noncriminal future. It is too early to say with confidence that he will no longer be tempted and perhaps fall, but he now knows that there are times when he is under pressure and poorly controlled, and that such periods may be precarious, in view of his criminal history and consequent tendency to recurrence. His growing awareness of these states may be of help as he realizes that he does not inevitably have to follow the old course which led him to prison. On the credit side is the fact that since his liberation four years ago, he has never relinquished a job. When he became depressed and failed, it was in a situation of genuine stress, brought about by continued unemployment and anxiety over his family. He could find no place to put his fund of energy. He learned from the one experience how much he valued what he had built and how painful it would be to lose it.

We have known Jacques B. for over six years, the first two when he was in prison. Though our aim was research, we did not hesitate to give both interpretation and suggestions when indicated and what he gained was a steady, consistent relationship. The contact has included interviews in the penitentiary, visits to his home, and office interviews with himself, his wife, and other family members. The value lay not so much in the number of interviews or their frequency, which varied with the need, but in the fact that the relationship was there and was meaningful; that the contact has never been broken and still exists.

CLINICAL EVALUATION

To evaluate the progress in Jacques B.'s criminal life, we will use five psychodynamic concepts that can serve as an index of change for better or worse in the course of a psychopathological state. These concepts encompass two opposite poles, allowing us to describe many shifts of equilibrium and disequilibrium. The concepts are not contradictory but, rather, complementary and interlocking. They are: increment-decrement; alloplasticity-autoplasticity; ego syntonia-ego dystonia; regression-progression; the development of object relations.

Increment and Decrement

In some mental illness, as in physical, there is an inherent tendency toward self-healing, and unless the disease process is too extensive, reparative mechanisms go into play. These lead to full restoration, or there may be incomplete healing with a permanent deficit or progressive deterioration of function. There is reason to believe that in certain psychopathological states, the reparatory mechanisms are such that an individual cannot only return to a previous state, but in the process of overcoming his illness acquire new strength previously existing only as a potential. This phenomenon is well known in physical medicine, where a disease process may be followed by immunity.

This gain or loss of capacity of an organism to respond to a stressful situation can be described as increment or decrement of function. The concept is useful for the understanding of the evolution of antisocial behavior. For many individuals, only one exposure to an experience with the law will serve as a permanent deterrent. The event, damaging as it may have been at the time, is an increment as it was followed by a curative learning experience which prevented repetition. Others, who are involved once in a similar criminal experience acquire a certain amount of temporary immunity, but there may be an eventual relapse. Such people are among those we call "episodic recidivists" (9). In the case of the persistent offender, though he eventually abates, for many years each criminal act is followed by an increment of criminal susceptibility. The criminality may be compared to an addictive process. Even this type of extreme susceptibility has its end. After many years of increasing, persistent criminality, the attraction toward crime diminishes and resistance develops.

This tendency can be seen in the police record itself, which may show either decreasing severity of offenses or the lengthening of crime-free periods with the passing of the years. These are significant observations; and when we find an individual record with such a trend, it indicates a decrement of criminality. For other offenders, however, the criminal record may grow not less but more severe. This increase does not necessarily correspond to an increment in criminality. Some offenders may continue to be severely criminal, but when studied psychologically, it can be seen that delinquent acting out becomes less and less appealing. Such criminals sometimes abate abruptly after committing their most serious offense.

The criminal record is, therefore, not necessarily a complete guide. For a more true indication of increase or decrease, we require a synthesis of all factors: the record, a psychological study, how the offender feels, how he sees himself now in comparison to what he was previously. We may then reach what appears to be a paradoxical judgment: that a man in his thirties whose criminality is overtly on the increase may be more and more depressed and anxious and experience a great deal of emotional discomfort not felt previously.

Increment and decrement are illustrated throughout Jacques B.'s criminal history. During adolescence he was fully involved in a polymorphous type of delinquency which included stealing, running way, and perverse sexuality. The one missing element was violence. In early maturity the criminality continued, was even augmented, but grew less random and with the defined aim of profit.

By the middle twenties, though he enjoyed the excitement of stealing, it was followed by depression and guilt and he began to find satisfaction in work. From then on each episode of stealing was succeeded by a decrement of criminality, manifested not only by the lapse of time between prison sentences but the lengthening periods of gainful work. In the last thefts for which he was imprisoned, at age, 26, he stole with the conscious aim of maintaining his home, and his latest episode shows most clearly the decrement in criminality. He broke down in a situation of stress, but this delinquent act, for which he was neither caught nor punished, was followed by what appears the greatest decrement in criminality so far. For the first time he stopped voluntarily before he was caught, and the suffering engendered by the delinquency has been a better deterrent than fear of punishment.

Autoplastic and Alloplastic Modes of Adaptation

Man, born in complete dependence, is of all creatures the one most able to achieve freedom of action and thought, to develop a variety of adaptive patterns and modes of behavior. Two of these, first described by Darwin and later brought into psychiatric usage by the psychoanalytic school, are called "autoplastic" and "alloplastic" modes. The autoplastic formation is characterized by an ability to change the self for better or worse, as a means of adapting to a changing life situation. The alloplastic mode is one where the individual seeks to change the environment as a way of adjustment. Normally, there is an interplay of autoplastic and alloplastic formations, one or the other predominating according to the situation and the need. There are personalities who show a dominance toward either alloplasticity or autoplasticity. Others have periods where they use mainly one or another solution; that is, under some conditions or during a certain mental or emotional state, they will employ almost exclusively an autoplastic or an alloplastic formation, or alternate rapidly from one to the other.

When we think of these modes of reaction and adaptation to life in regard to socialization, we can define the healthy individual as one capable of changing himself when necessary without interfering unduly with others, and who is also able to change the environment to achieve justifiable individual or social aims. In the complex evolution of a criminal career, it is not surprising that the balance between autoplastic and alloplastic formations undergoes many shifts and that there is seldom what may be called a harmonious equilibrium. In early life, the child who later becomes a criminal usually resorts to alloplastic adaptation rather than making necessary inner changes. However, by the time criminality abates, the balance between autoplasticity and alloplasticity is likely to have been reversed.

These concepts can be carried a step further to take into account mental activity, including the content of thought, fantasy, and dreams. The quality of the thinking may be autoplastic or alloplastic with interrelationship and interplay from one to another. In a criminal career, therefore, it is important to study not only the mode of physical adaptation and reaction, but the mode of thinking, fantasy, and dreams.

Jacques B.'s major reaction formations and defenses in infancy were compulsivity and overactivity. By age six, he was an antisocial child who attacked the world as his mode of dealing with internal and external conflicts. In adolescence, his delinquent acting out grew more organized and rational. However, by the end of adolescence, two types of alloplastic formations had emerged: compulsive delinquency and compulsive work. In early maturity, work acquired great meaning, and though he remained a delinquent, being a skilled worker was a rewarding experience. Thus, his alloplasticity acquired a new direction so that while from age 15 to 25 there was mainly delinquency, following this there was mainly work. At present Jacques B.'s dominant mode of adaptation remains generally alloplastic, but autoplastic formations are taking shape.

During his latency and early adolescence, autoplastic mechanisms were largely suppressed or displaced, as shown by the absence of sublimation, the lack of tolerance to frustration, and the inability to withstand ambivalent relations. The aggression was mainly directed outward rather than against the self. The appearance of autoplastic formations, such as depression, a sense of suffering, and a need for object relations, first became apparent in adolescence, when he became attached to a teacher. Through this man, he gave up some of his alloplasticity and, as a result, was able to learn intellectually and to some extent emotionally. This coexistence of alloplastic and autoplastic reactions became more marked from this time. He gradually gained some satisfaction and relief in changing himself instead of always fighting the environment; there were solutions in fantasy and in the beginnings of an ego ideal. For example, when his girl waited for him while he was in prison, he responded with a desire to protect her instead of, as previously, to profit from her. This important experience at age 25 made him realize that transforming himself could give more contentment than attacking and exploiting. Progressively, he has learned that a powerful way of adaptation is to make internal changes.

The quality of Jacques B.'s thinking has also changed in the process. As a child, he saw himself as the center of the universe. This was succeeded by his feeling that he was surrounded by a hostile world which he must deal with aggressively. The content of his thinking and of his fantasy, therefore, was retaliatory. There has been a modification into what can be called normal aspirations, with hopes and plans for himself and his family which he knows he must earn.

Ego-syntonia and Ego-dystonia

As prevalently used, "ego-syntonia" refers to a condition consistent with the ego ideal, or with consciously held ideals, or a condition where the ego and superego are in agreement. "Ego-dystonia" conveys the contrary, an emotional state unacceptable to the ego. We employ these terms in a broader sense, and describe as ego-syntonic any mechanism whether normal or pathological, any reaction formation, and any behavior which gives an individual a sense of ego strength and security. A condition or behavior which produces the contrary would be felt as ego-dystonic.

Symptoms and pathological formations which may in themselves be regarded as ego-dystonic are at certain times, for a given individual within the changing and varying circumstances of his life, experienced as ego-syntonic. In a different context, the same formations may become ego-dystonic. As an example, a compulsive state which at first gives energy, a sense of power and accomplishment, and therefore of well-being, may eventually become self-defeating and produce ego dissatisfaction. A feeling of strength can in time, by a process of reversal determined by psychological forces finding their roots in the personality structure and in the milieu, be transformed into its opposite, weakness and failure.

Exhibitionism was for Jacques B. a means to attain an ego-syntonic state. This exhibitionism, which often took the form of delinquency and got him into trouble. nevertheless provided pleasure and a sense of well-being. Instead of concealing his misconduct, he enjoyed parading it, at the risk of severe punishment. The public exposure involved became in itself a kind of exhibitionism, and contributed to his feeling of power. He felt like an acknowledged athlete, a "champion," to use his own words. Recalling this period 15 years later, he still experiences a certain pleasure. No matter what other aims were served by his misconduct at school, the maintaining of an ego-syntonic state was one of them.

An attempt to use this mechanism, which failed to achieve its objective, took place some years later when he was in prison. It occurred during the interview described in the case history, when he was very angry with his wife for her infidelity and he tried to overcome his depression by boasting about his sexual exploits, flaunting all he had done that he himself considered wrong and perverse and that also would shock the interviewer, who would then be convinced of his manifest superiority in sexual misconduct. It was a virtuoso piece of exhibitionism, but in the course of the account he grew suddenly depressed; the pleasure did not even last the telling. The acting out and the exhibitionism, which went hand in hand, no longer contributed to his well-being; and what was ego-syntonic once was now felt as ego-dystonic. It is unlikely that he would ever again display his adolescent polymorphous sexuality as a means of exhibitionism and shock. If he had to describe this part of his life, it would probably give him pain and and embarrassment, and it would be in a therapeutic situation.

Regression and Progression

The emotional movement involved in the return to past stages and feelings, the revival of more primitive modes of action and reaction, is called "regression." The ensuing movement forward to more mature levels from a more primitive state is described as "progression." Progression and regression in an individual can be seen as aspects either of health or disease. Regression is not necessarily a symptom of a pathological state. Viewed in the context of a specific situation, whether of short or long duration, the capacity to return at will to more primitive levels may be an asset promoting health and spontaneity. Normal people switch rapidly and easily in the course of daily life. A well-adjusted adult can share his play with children as if he were a child, and yet with facility return to himself as an adult. In physical illness a certain amount of regression is not only permitted but encouraged. A person normally self-sufficient should allow others to care for him without anxiety or insecurity. A degree of emotional as well as physical regression helps him to recover.

On the other hand, regression may accompany an abnormal state, either transient or prolonged. In such cases the presence of regression is an important index of ongoing psychopathology. A state of regression is a point of departure from which one can go forward, remain fixed, or recede even further. Regression may be so severe that the individual will remain in that condition permanently, or make only a partial recovery. Some return to their previous state, while others will do more, they will recover with an increment. Certain pathological formations are symptomatic of a lack of progression rather than a true regression.

The concept of regression and progression has value in the study of a criminal career, and the late maturation of the personality. We find in these men who show some capacity for self-healing many movements of regression and progression, much travelling back and forth in the psyche. Regression-progression can be seen as a dynamic counterpart of the descriptive concept of increment and decrement already discussed.

What is of note in the development of Jacques B.'s character from early childhood to the present is the slow process of growth throughout, his difficulty in advancing from one stage to the next, and in particular the delay in acquiring social values. The persistence of infantile modes continued in latency and were prolonged well into manhood. To the extent that he has overcome immature responses, we see a forward, if fluctuating movement. His whole process of maturation is characterized by a gradual progression with frequent periods of regression, showing strongly entrenched persistence of old infantile patterns only gradually replaced.

In analyzing Jacques B.'s criminal career, we note the appearance in late adolescence of islands of normal, acceptable behavior when work replaced stealing. This has been reinforced in the twenties and markedly so since his marriage. These periods are undoubtedly a progression from his previous aimless, compulsive, delinquent activity. More and more his gains are solidly established. In analyzing his last three episodes of stealing, we observed that on each occasion a return to criminality coincided with a state of mind in which for a period he abandoned newly acquired values to return to old patterns. In following the movement forward and back in Jacques B.'s development, it can be seen that delinquency in latency was a reflection of a lack of progression, while his latest episode is an expression of a temporary relapse, that is, a regression followed, however, by a greater progression.

Development of Object Relations

The importance of object relations in the early formative years has already been mentioned. The quality of the relationship between a child and parental figures predetermines and modifies the type of relationships he will build in later life.

The type of relationship which shows least maturity is one where an adult can establish contact only for narcissistic pleasure and self-gain. The mature adult can integrate his own needs and pleasures in complex compromises, taking into account what is due to others. He is also able to sustain within a relationship a certain amount of frustration and pain which is the price of maintaining it. As further evidence of integration in the development of object relations, a mature individual, whether or not he plays an active role in society, is concerned with social values. He can maintain a flexible, changing, but responsible relationship with individuals and with society, which gives satisfaction and security, but also demands some suffering and denial, entailing a certain amount of insecurity and loss. When, through lack of sound object relations in early childhood, an individual fails to acquire an equilibrium between id, ego, and superego, his major means of overcoming this deficiency is through a remedial relationship from which he learns. This kind of relationship may be acquired in life or in a therapeutic situation.

The character and quality of Jacques B.'s object relations and their evolution are demonstrated in his changing behavior and attitude, first to his mother, and later to his wife. In early infancy he learned to use his mother as an object to be exploited and, when necessary, defied; he nevertheless felt that he loved her. By the time he reached puberty he felt quite consciously that he could and should have power over her. Toward the father, with whom he identified as the omnipotent controlling figure, there was fear and rivalry. This is shown at the time of his father's desertion, when along with blame and anger there was a conviction that he, the oldest son, should now be master of the home.

His method of controlling was to alternate between misconduct and sweetness, and he managed people who were made captive by his charm, yet were defeated in their efforts to help him. The same attitude was carried over later when he began to exploit women for profit, and at the same time found a mother figure in them. To be a pimp and gigolo were means of governing and controlling and yet remaining dependent and kept.

A genuine change occurred when he met the girl who later became his wife. Here he discovered a new possibility, that between people there could be a mutual give and take. He developed a sense of belonging, and with it, gradually some social values. In prison, out of fear of losing her, he had to learn how to deal with ambivalent feelings and he further consolidated the relationship. Since then his feeling toward his wife has deepened and become a crucial part of his emotional and social development. When he is depressed, under stress, she is a source of strength. When the stress becomes too severe, he begins to hurt her, as shown in his last experience, when he rejected her attempts to keep him from criminality. He has learned, though late, how to achieve a solid human relationship with a woman where he is the defender and protector and which includes the ability to withstand negative feelings.

Similar changes in object relations can be traced in regard to male figures. There was great aggressivity and hatred of the father expressed in his own phrase, "What is a bad man is my father—not me." Moreover, he profited from men as a homosexual. His experience with a teacher in adolescence gave him some intimation of what a good father could be. It was in the course, however, of his deepening relationship to his wife and children that he learned to reverse to some extent his opinion of his own father. He replaced the picture of the all-bad father with a truer image. In this process, the opposite picture of an all-perfect mother was more realistically seen, so that he now has a better balance. His increasing ability to identify with male figures is shown as well in his capacity for sustained work and in his acceptance of some supervision and authority, which includes a social code.

SELF-HEALING AND THE CRIMINAL PROCESS

The psychodynamic formulation of a criminal career is more than the sum of the many separate, repetitive criminal acts which make up the total of that history. It contains not only the history of the delinquent acting out and its psychogenesis, but goes beyond to include the socializing energies potentially at the disposal of the individual.

Psychoanalysis lays stress on the genetic reconstruction of pathological formations, but the exposure of their roots is only the first stage of the therapeutic technique. This return to the past permits the uprooting of fixations which interfere with development; when these fixations are out of the way, normal growth is able to follow its course. We may use as a metaphor the current of a river held back by the debris it carries with it, which piles up, clogging and impeding its course. The obstruction can be swept away by the power of the stream, or reinforce and entrench itself so that external intervention is the only means of liberating the waters. No matter how the flow of water is restored, its sudden release, with consequent danger of flooding, may create new impediments further down the stream, which again will either dam the waters, be swept away by the force of the current, or be removed only by outside intervention. In somewhat the same fashion, both the development and the neutralization of pathological formations are an intricate series of doings and undoings and redoings, analysis being one of the means of freeing the personality.

To describe an undoing procedure which takes place in life without therapeutic intervention, we have no better term than emotional self-healing. The history of Jacques B., the changes taking place between the onset of his delinquency and the time we first saw him, that is, from about age 6 to 26, demonstrates this process well. His development shows many similarities to the changes taking place in psychotherapy, one of the most marked lying in the fact that he has slowly changed himself, at first less consciously, but with growing awareness. His self-healing parallels changes occurring in therapy, such as movement forward and backward, regression being a step back from which he takes a new and further advance, and the reorganization of the balance of his mechanisms of defense.

The process of self-healing takes place with a certain amount of awareness, involving a certain degree of conscious change so that an individual may at times resist change or foster it. The fact that self-healing goes on without the help of a therapeutic relationship and interpretation from another raises an important question: Is there a substitute or an alternative for the therapist?

We suggest that the surrounding world, the individual's constant clash and interaction with it, plays the role of the other in a therapeutic dialogue. Jacques B. was able to use the external world, its pressures and opportunities, in a remedial, self-correcting way. When he used reality testing constructively, it was for him an effective, meaningful, therapeutic interpretation. His destructive use of reality, bringing with it failure and punishment, provided a therapeutic interpretation when the consequences of his acts forced on him a better reality testing. From his successes and failures he eventually developed a truer perception of reality.

The very reality testing which in the end served therapeutic purposes was in itself impaired during Jacques B.'s early formative years, blocking his progress. In his childhood it was impossible to reach normal socialization and it took decades to gain what the average child does in the first few years. Yet he made use of this defective tool and he improved it with use. With regard to an individual like Jacques B., it can be said that no matter how pathological his behavior and personality, he still lives in the world and it is still at his disposal, even if badly used. In the behavior disorders, reality testing may be distorted and poorly directed, but as most energies are channelled outside, an exchange, a balance between outer reality and the inner world, remains the fundamental characteristic of this pathology. An individual with a behavior disorder differs from the deteriorating schizophrenic who turns inward and builds a world of his own. The external world is not available for reality testing.

Self-healing is by no means exclusive to the abatement of persistent criminality, but is a process that takes place in pathological conditions with a potential for recovery. That the capacity for self-healing depends to an important degree on the capacity for reality testing is demonstrated by the process known as "mourning work," which begins when the mourner recognizes that the object is lost forever. Only after this acceptance can healing begin.

If we have found it necessary to seek a dynamic explanation to understand the evolution of habitual criminality, it is because we are confronted with a lengthy development which, nevertheless, terminates. We have attempted to delineate its course with the help of psychiatric formulations and analytic concepts, but this is not the only approach. The problem must be examined from many aspects and in the contexts of other theories. From the point of view of theories of the learning process, an interpretation of our material—noting Jacques B.'s low capacity to learn in childhood and his increased ability as he grew older—may be seen not so much in terms of psychic development but as an impairment of his learning function. With regard to the changes taking place in Jacques B., an explanation arising from dynamic psychiatry or from learning theories may not be in contradiction, as pointed out by Alexander (2).

We are, however, still left with a basic question, regardless of whether our theory is analytic: Why, with a normal potential, was Jacques B. unable to learn in the first place? In looking for an explanation of this fundamental problem, we do not exclude hereditary organic and constitutional factors; and if in the case of Jacques B. we stress the emotional development, it is because his criminal career can be explained, at least largely, in terms of a pathological personality formation.

CHRONOLOGICAL AND EMOTIONAL TIME IN THE CRIMINAL PROCESS: THERAPEUTIC AND LEGAL IMPLICATIONS

That a man is perpetually changing, yet retains his sense of always being himself, which includes what he has been, what he is now, and an awareness that in the future he will still be himself with some change, is a truism that in the past pertained more to philosophy than to psychiatry. Classic psychiatry was little concerned with time as a perception, and confined itself to isolating certain syndromes which were more likely to occur at different life stages than at others. Hebephrenia and melancholia are two examples of illnesses associated with two periods of life.

Modern schools of psychiatry have broadened the concept of time as a living dimension. In dealing with emotional relations, psychoanalysis has involved itself with time through its clinical methods, such as free association and the reconstruction of the past. In psychoanalysis, a basic postulate is that the patient is to-day the end product, the culmination of his total past; and that the changes taking place in the therapeutic process can modify the future. Past, present, and future are, therefore, part of a living chain.

The phenomenological school of psychiatry, with its emphasis on "being-in-the-world," offers an approach to time as a continuity which was at first more philosophical than clinical, laying great stress on a dynamic perception of time, to the ways in which it is experienced, and describes mental processes in an emotional time continuity not unlike psychonanalysis, the emphasis being on the living present which contains the past. The phenomenological school, which derived from the existentialist philosophy, has greatly enlarged our knowledge of the psychology of time (5).

These approaches place both normal and pathological processes in a time dimension which is broader and goes far beyond elapsed chronological time. Time becomes a dimension in itself, as well as a continuity. We cannot go backward physically in time and regain the lost years or make the future happen more quickly or more slowly. Emotional time, however, allows movement in all directions, past and future; and it is in the inner reality of this time continuity which has its effect on outer reality that we must study a human being.

These remarks on time and their clinical and social significance are relevant to the many changes which took place in Jacques B.'s life. At age 34, when he committed his last, uncaught offense, he contained within himself his whole past, the disturbed child of six and the delinquent adolescent. Nevertheless, at 30 he was neither the child nor the adolescent, but a man whose diagnosis and prognosis were not the same as they would have been at an earlier period. To foresee the direction of future change, it was essential to evaluate the transformation taking place from his childhood to age 34, to be aware that he had in a sense become a different self which yet encompassed his previous selves. Taking all this into account, our prognosis at age 30 was favorable, with some reservations.

Such a prognosis would not have held much water in a legal judgment, which is concerned with the number of years of criminal life and the number of convictions. In our contact with Jacques B., one of our main problems has been the discrepancy between legal and psychiatric judgment. When Jacques B. lapsed temporarily into criminality in his last offense, we were only too uncomfortably aware of the consequences had he been detected. The number of years spent in criminal activity and in prison would have affected the sentence he received far more than the kind of progress he was achieving in his emotional time continuum, which obeys other laws than those of chronological time. We could not wish him to succeed in his criminality, though fortunately it involved no violence or physical injury. Nevertheless, a harsh sentence would not necessarily have best served what should be the two major aims of justice—the protection of the community and the rehabilitation of the offender. The ideal consequence would have been for Jacques to be caught, tried, and if found guilty, sentenced.

We hold that justice should not be bypassed, even to achieve a desirable therapeutic outcome. Contrary to the generally held legal view that severity deters, our opinion is that one of the foundations of social deterrence is that the more certain an offender is that he will be detected and punished, the more likely he is to desist from crime. A proviso is that it be a truly just and humane sentence, based on the full knowledge of an individual's history. In the case of Jacques B., for instance, probation would have been the sentence of choice, one clear-cut condition being that he remain in contact with our research group. In the legal and social setting in which Jacques B. would have been sentenced, the odds that he would receive such a disposition were much against him. In his own way, he seems to have understood that probation would have been a just sentence, as shown by the fact that since this relapse two years ago he has in a sense voluntarily put himself on probation to us.

The whole course of Jacques B.'s development confirms our belief that cooperation between law and the sciences of human behavior is a crucial necessity. It illustrates one of the central problems in dealing with individuals like him, whom we call primary delinquents. In his childhood and adolescence, he was placed in custodial institutions without treatment. In one sense the law was lenient, not to say lax. It allowed his delinquency to take its own path without the therapeutic intervention which would have required skilled professional help and a difficult struggle for Jacques before he could succeed, if at all, in making changes within himself at that age. In his adult life, however, when he was able to change himself considerably in the course of a painful self-healing process, and when he ultimately and willingly accepted help from outside, the law grew progressively more severe. We are casting blame neither on law nor psychiatry for this illogic, but it is time that the administration of justice came to grips with the problem. Criminality is a social disorder which demands the concerted efforts of many disciplines, but the final responsibility remains with the law. No rational solution is possible in the absence of a sound penal philosophy based on understanding of the criminal process as seen in individuals, and of criminality as a phenomenon of man and his society.

SUMMARY

Criminal process has been studied in the light of one individual history. The natural history of criminality and its outcome have been traced from childhood to maturity. We have postulated that a certain type of criminal behavior is a pathological process and to retrace this evolution is an essential first step toward intervening with the aim of interrupting or modifying its course. Five psychiatric concepts were used in this particular case in order to identify and understand reparatory mechanisms which lead to a degree of self-healing. The inference is that with a fuller knowledge of the criminal process, a rational treatment approach may be possible, which would accelerate the existing potential for growth and for healthy personal and social adaptation. This study has legal as well as psychiatric implications, a significant one resting in the fact that the persistent offender may have a good prognosis precisely at the period of his life when the law tends to be most severe.

REFERENCES

1. Aichhorn, A. *Wayward Youth*. New York: Meridian Books Inc., 1955.
2. Alexander, F. The dynamics of psychotherapy in the light of learning theory. *Amer. J. Psychiat.* 5:441-448, 1963.
3. *Annual Reports of the Commissioner of Penitentiaries*, 1935 to 1960 incl., Queen's Printer, Ottawa.
4. Bettelheim, B. *Love Is Not Enough*. Glencoe (Ill.): The Free Press, 1950.
5. Binswanger, L. *Being-In-The-World*. New York: Basic Books, Inc., 1963.
6. *Canadian Census, 1961*. Dominion Bureau of Statistics, Cat. 92-525. Ottawa: Queen's Printer, 1961.
7. Cormier, B. M., Kennedy, M., Sangowicz, J., and Trottier, M. Presentation of a basic classification for clinical work and research in criminology. *Can. J. Corrections* 4:21-34, 1959.
8. ———. The natural history of criminality and some tentative hypotheses on its abatement. 4:35-49, 1959.
9. Cormier, B. M., *et al.* Delinquent Acting Out, Episodic Recidivism and the Psychological State. Unpublished paper, 1964.
10. Friedlander, K. *The Psychoanalytical Approach to Juvenile Delinquency*. London: Routledge & Kegan Paul Ltd., 1947.
11. Glueck, S., and Glueck, E. T. *One Thousand Juvenile Delinquents*. Cambridge: Harvard University Press, 1934.
12. ———. *Juvenile Delinquents Grow Up*. New York: The Commonwealth Fund, 1942.
13. ———. *Unravelling Juvenile Delinquency*. Cambridge: Harvard University Press, 1950.
14. Grant, J. D., and Grant, M. Q. A group dynamics approach to the treatment of nonconformists in the Navy. *Ann. Amer. Acad. Political and Social Science* 332:126-135, 1959.
15. Healy, W., and Bronner, A. F. *Delinquents and Criminals. Their Making and Unmaking*. New York: The Macmillan Company, 1926.
16. Johnson, A. M., and Azurek, S. A. Genesis of anti-social acting

out in children and adults. *Psychoanal. Quart.* 21:323-343, 1952.

17. Karpman, B. *Case Studies in the Psychopathology of Crime* (4 vols.). Washington, D.C.: Medical Science Press, 1948.
18. Mailloux, N., and Lavllée, C. Les aberrations du développement psycho-social et la personnalité du délinquant. *Le Cahier de Contributions à l'Étude des Sciences de l'Homme* (Montreal) 5:138-157, 1962.
19. Minkowski, E. Le Temps Vécu. *Collection de l'Évolution Psychiatrique.* Paris, 1933.
20. Quêtelet, A. *Recherches sur le penchant au crime aux différents âges* (2nd ed.). Bruxelles: Hayes, 1833.
21. ———. A Treatise on Man and the Development of his Faculties. Translated from the French, 1842.
22. Redl, F., and Wineman, D. *The Aggressive Child.* Glencoe (Ill.): The Free Press, 1957.
23. Russon, G. W. A design for clinical classification of offenders. *Can. J. Corrections* 3:179-188, 1962
24. Schmideberg, M. Maturation and integration of the superego in the treatment of delinquents. *Arch. of Criminal Psychodynamics* 1:101-110, 1955.
25. Sellin, T. Recidivism and maturation. *National Probation and Parole Assoc. J.* 1:241-250, 1958.
26. Shaw, C. R. *The Jack-Roller.* Philadelphia: Albert Saifer, 1930.
27. Sullivan, C. E., Grant, J. D., and Grant, M. Q. The development of interpersonal maturity: Applications to delinquency. *Psychiatry* 20:373-385, 1957.
28. Talhurst, G. Comments on the Application of Russon's Design for Clinical Classification of Offenders. Paper presented at Canadian Congress of Corrections, Winnipeg, June 1963.

Psychiatric Treatment as an Alternative to Imprisonment

KENNETH G. GRAY

Until well into the twentieth century, the relationship of psychiatry to criminal law in Canada followed a pattern which was similar to that which prevailed in England, the United States of America, and other common-law countries. Both medical and legal writers were preoccupied with the legal rules governing insanity as a defense. Psychiatrists attacked the M'Naghten Rules and lawyers defended them. There were attempts, which persist today, to achieve a legal rule which would differentiate accurately the guilty from the ill.

The subject is of diminishing importance with the declining use of capital punishment. This is due in part to the increase in commutation of the death sentence by the government of Canada. Another factor is the classification of murder into capital or noncapital murder in Section 202A of the Criminal Code. A con-

I have drawn extensively upon the experience and data of my colleagues on the staff of the Toronto Psychiatric Hospital and the Department of Psychiatry of the University of Toronto, particularly the following: Mr. V. Hartman, Chief Social Worker, Forensic Clinic, Toronto Psychiatric Hospital; Dr. H. C. Hutchison, Chief Psychologist, Forensic Clinic, Toronto Psychiatric Hospital; Dr. J. W. Mohr, Research Associate, Forensic Clinic, Toronto Psychiatric Hospital; Dr. M. D. Tuchtie, Psychiatrist in Charge, Forensic In-Patient Service, Toronto Psychiatric Hospital; Dr. R. E. Turner, Director, Forensic Clinic, Toronto Psychiatric Hospital. I am indebted to Mrs. J. J. Veyvara of the Department of Psychiatry of the University of Toronto for preparing the manuscript for publication.

viction for capital murder results in a sentence of death and a conviction for noncapital murder results in a sentence of life imprisonment.

A decline in capital punishment is likely to result in a decline in the number of cases in which insanity is pleaded as a defense. The reason is related to the outcome of a successful plea of insanity. The Criminal Code provides that a person who is acquitted on the ground of insanity is to be held at the pleasure of the lieutenant-governor, which means, in our constitutional practice, at the pleasure of the government of the province in which the trial is held. It has been a long-established policy that such persons are committed to a mental hospital and are seldom released, even if they recover. Counsel for an accused person is unlikely to plead insanity, leading to custody for life in a mental hospital, if the alternative is a sentence of imprisonment with a fixed date of termination.

The reduction in the use of insanity as a defense would have resulted in a diminishing use of psychiatry in criminal trials were it not for another development—an increase in psychiatric examinations in relation to sentence. This is relatively new. It was not used extensively until after World War II.

As psychiatrists and psychologists were requested with increasing frequency to examine criminal offenders in relation to sentence, it became apparent that a proportion of the offenders were likely to benefit from treatment. Initially, treatment came to be provided for the offender who was certifiably mentally ill and who could be treated in a mental hospital. At a later stage, treatment in an out-patient clinic was provided for some offenders who could be put on probation without undue risk for the community. During this period psychiatric services were developing in some of the juvenile courts but a discussion of these is not included here.

The remainder of this chapter describes the facilities for examination and treatment of adult offenders available at the Toronto Psychiatric Hospital in cooperation with the Department of Psychiatry of the University of Toronto.

The forensic services in Toronto began in the year 1925. The statute which provided for the establishment of the Toronto Psychiatric Hospital contained a section authorizing the admission of a patient for mental examination upon the order of a judge or magistrate. This section is still in force. On the authority of this section, 4877 persons have been admitted to the hospital by the courts for examination.

There is no separate ward or unit for these patients. Patients admitted through the courts are admitted to the general wards of the hospital and are not distinguished in any way from other patients in the hospital. The service is available for both men and women.

The hospital is maintained by the government of Ontario and is affiliated with the Department of Psychiatry of the University of Toronto. The hospital is staffed and equipped to provide complete physical and mental investigation, with consultation services available from other departments of the Faculty of Medicine. A patient who is received through the court remains in the hospital on an average of about four weeks.

It will be seen in Figure 1 that patients so admitted are charged with a variety of criminal offenses. In addition, 30.3 percent of the patients were charged with "suspected of being mentally ill."

The disposal of the cases is shown in Figure 2. It will be noted that 43.1 percent were certified to an Ontario (mental) hospital. These were the patients who were certifiably mentally ill or mentally defective. When a patient is certified and transferred to an Ontario hospital, a notation is made as to whether or not the charge against him was withdrawn. If the charge is not withdrawn the patient returns to court to stand trial when he is discharged from the Ontario hospital.

Of the 798 cases, 40.1 percent were returned to court. These patients would be tried for their offenses. In each case a report is sent to the court containing a summary of the findings in the Toronto Psychiatric Hospital. These reports are frequently used by the judges and magistrates in relation to sentence. If the patient is sentenced to imprisonment, the report may be sent to the penal institution. If the case is deemed suitable for outpatient treatment, the court may impose suspended sentence and probation with the condition that the patient report to the outpatient clinic for treatment.

Also in Figure 2 it may be noted that 16.8 percent of the court cases were discharged directly from the Toronto Psychiatric Hospital

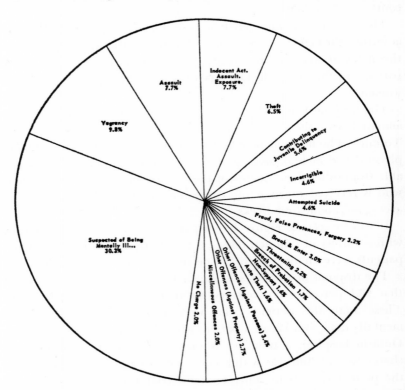

FIGURE 1. *University of Toronto, Department of Psychiatry, and the Toronto Psychiatric Hospital Forensic Inpatient Service, 1950– 1959, nature of offense, 798 cases discharged.*

to their homes. With the approval of the court, this is done in the case of a person who is not certifiably mentally ill or defective and where the charge is withdrawn. Any such person who is in need of further treatment will be referred to the outpatient clinic.

Figure 3 illustrates what happens to those patients in Figure 2 who comprise the 40.1 percent who were returned to court. It will be noted that 30.3 percent were placed on probation, 13.3 percent were given suspended sentence, and in 17.8 percent the charge was dismissed. These three groups total 61.4 percent. That is, 61.4 per-

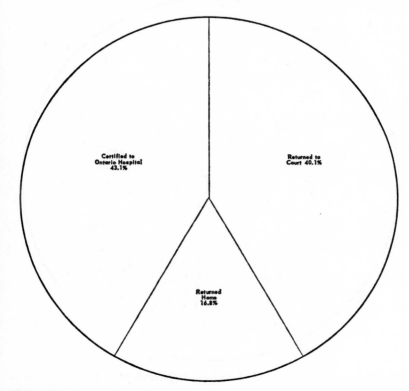

FIGURE 2. *University of Toronto, Department of Psychiatry, and the Toronto Psychiatric Hospital Forensic Inpatient Service, 1950–1959, disposal of 798 cases.*

cent of all the cases returned to court were not sentenced to imprisonment.

The procedure which began in 1925 for remand by courts to the hospital has continued without interruption to this day. It should be emphasized that these examinations are carried out not primarily to formulate an opinion about fitness to stand trial or a defense of insanity but rather for the purpose of providing a report in relation to sentence of a convicted person. It has now been established that

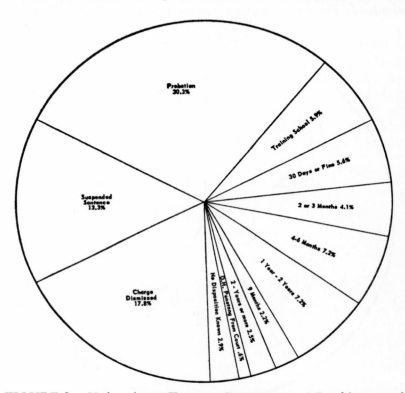

FIGURE 3. *University of Toronto, Department of Psychiatry, and the Toronto Forensic Inpatient Service, 1950–1959, disposal of 320 cases returned to court.*

a proportion of convicted persons may benefit from psychiatric treatment as an alternative to imprisonment and for a substantial number it is feasible to provide such treatment as an alternative to imprisonment without undue risk to society.

Until 1956 there was one serious lack in the treatment facilities.

There was no difficulty in arranging treatment in an Ontario (mental) hospital if the person was certifiably mentally ill or defective. Outpatient treatment was a different matter. The hospital was not adequately staffed to provide outpatient treatment for adult offenders, and there was understandable reluctance to accommodate them in clinics established for other types of patients.

In 1956 this defect was remedied when the government of Ontario established a special clinic for the diagnosis and treatment of adult offenders. The statutory authority for the clinic is contained in section 23 of the Psychiatric Hospitals Act which reads as follows:

1. There shall be a division of the Toronto Psychiatric Hospital to be known as the Forensic Clinic of the Toronto Psychiatric Hospital.
2. There shall be a director of the Clinic.
3. A judge or magistrate may order any person who is before him charged with or convicted of any offense to attend the Clinic for physical or mental examination, diagnosis, or treatment.
4. An order under subsection 3 shall not be made until the judge or magistrate has ascertained from the director of the Clinic that the services of the Clinic are available to the person named in the order.
5. The director of the Clinic may in his discretion report all or any part of the information compiled by the Clinic to
   (a) the judge or magistrate who made the order
   (b) an inspector
   (c) the person examined or
   (d) any person who, in the opinion of the director, has a *bona fide* interest in the person examined.

When the clinic was established by the government of Ontario in 1956 there was no information available to guide its founders. It was hoped that the clinic would provide a service for the courts by the examination of adult offenders and treatment for suitable cases. It was also hoped that through affiliation with the Department of Psychiatry of the University of Toronto, the clinic would be a center for teaching and research.

The clinic began as a pilot project, with a small professional staff and limited facilities. All three objectives—service for the courts, teaching, and research—have met with success. The staff of the clinic now includes three full-time psychiatrists, three part-time psychiatrists, four psychologists, and four social workers. There are four medical practitioners in full-time attendance at the clinic who are qualifying to become specialists in psychiatry. There is a full-time research assistant. The clinic is used as a teaching center by various departments of the university.

During 1962, 525 patients were seen, of whom 326 were new cases. The new cases are sent for investigation and assessment; of these a number are deemed to be suitable for treatment. Treatment may continue in some cases for many months, hence a caseload of patients in treatment is constantly being built up.

Statistics about the number of patients seen during 1962 appear in Table I. Detailed information is included in Table II about patients

TABLE I. *Forensic Clinic, Toronto Psychiatric Hospital, 1962*

	Male	Female	Total
A. No. of patients carried over from month of December, 1961	82	7	89
B. No. of new patients in 1962	287	39	326
C. No. of patients from previous years (i.e., 1956, 1957, 1958, 1959, 1960, and 1961) seen in 1962 in addition to those carried over from month of December, 1961	96	14	110
	465	60	525

attending the clinic in 1962. Information about the age and sex of new patients during 1962 is contained in Table III. The clinical diagnoses of the new cases attending during 1962 are shown in Tables IV and V.

Patients referred by the courts are charged with a variety of criminal offenses. About one-half are charged with sex offenses. This is probably due in part to the origin of the clinic. It came into being

TABLE II. *Forensic Clinic, Toronto Psychiatric Hospital, 1962*

Total number of attendances in 1962	4005
(An attendance is a visit to the clinic by the patient, a relative, or person on his behalf.)	
Total number of interviews to comply with methods of Division of Medical Statistics and community Mental Health Services, Department of Health, Ontario	4445
(An interview is a person to person interview between a patient and any member of the professional staff, or between a person or relative on behalf of the patient and any member of the professional staff, regardless of length of duration.)	
Total number of clinic personnel sessions	6042
(A personnel session is considered as one hour, or part of an hour of the professional staff member's time in interviewing the patient, i.e., a patient seen for testing by a psychologist for three hours with one hour for scoring tests would count only as one "interview," but would count as four "clinic sessions.")	
Total number of failed appointments	572
(Percentage of failed appointments as against actual attendances: 14.28 percent.)	

as a result of a widespread public demand in Ontario for the provision of treatment facilities for sexually deviated persons.

Mention has been made of a full-time research associate whose services are provided by the government of Ontario. The research associate is not a psychiatrist and is not associated with the diagnosis and treatment of individual patients. This has proved an additional stimulus to the research program, and professional journals contain the findings of a considerable number of research projects.

The nature and scope of the researches are developing with the increasing experience of the research staff and the stabilization of some of the research techniques. For example, in some of the more

TABLE III. *Forensic Clinic, Toronto Psychiatric Hospital, age and sex of new patients during 1962*

	Male	Female	Total
16–19 years	81	9	90
20–24 years	60	6	66
25–29 years	40	6	46
30–34 years	35	4	39
35–39 years	25	9	34
40–49 years	30	2	32
50 and over	16	3	19
	287	39	326

TABLE IV. *Forensic Clinic, Toronto Psychiatric Hospital, clinical diagnoses of new patients attended during 1962*

Schizophrenic disorders	6
Involutional melancholia	2
Paranoia and paranoid states	1
Anxiety reaction	2
Neurotic depressive reaction	1
Psychoneurotic disorders (other and unspecified)	9
Psychophysiologic disorders	6
Disorders of character, behavior, and intelligence (see Table V)	212
Personality trait disorders	52
Alcoholism	5
Primary childhood behaviors, conduct disturbance	2
Mental deficiency	5
Acute situational maladjustment	4
Simple adult maladjustment	1
Epilepsy	2
Undiagnosed (not seen by doctor)	9
No psychiatric diagnoses found	7
Total	326

recent projects the services of a lawyer have been enlisted. At this time one lawyer is spending full time in one of the projects. The investigations are beginning to extend beyond the patients seen in the clinic and have encompassed a survey in collaboration with the staff of the Ontario Hospital Penetanguishene of the criminally in-

TABLE V. *Forensic Clinic, Toronto Psychiatric Hospital, clinical diagnoses of new patients attended during 1962, disorders of character, behavior, and intelligence*

Pathological personality	2
Schizoid personality	4
Paranoid personality	1
Antisocial personality	20
Inadequate personality	14
Asocial personality	6
Sexual deviation	
General sexual deviation	3
Homosexuality	51
Exhibitionism	35
Pedophilia	43
Sado-masochism	5
Voyeurism	9
Transvestism	3
Fetishism	4
Incest	4
Multiple sex perversions	1
Bestiality	2
Other and unspecified	5
Total	212

sane who are confined in that hospital. Another survey has dealt with the sex offenders in some of the penal institutions in Ontario. Another study is concerned with a personality study of young offenders from 16 to 20 years of age in the adult courts of metropolitan Toronto.

The clinic has collected voluminous information about all types of sexual deviation including pedophilia. The subject of pedophilia has been selected to illustrate in some detail the work of the forensic clinic in the field of sexual deviation. The sexual molestation of young children is a type of deviation which arouses great public concern.

The basic measurement in the follow-up of offenders is the rate of recidivism. The general recidivism rate for sexual offenders is low, lying between 13 percent and 17 percent. Exhibitionism and homosexual pedophilia show the highest rate of about 20 to 30 percent. Differences in prediction also depend upon the previous criminal record. Offenders with previous convictions for sex offenses are about three times more likely to commit another offense than first offenders.

It is apparent from the findings in the clinic that there is little value in quoting recidivism for sexual offenders as a group. It is essential to establish the recidivism rate in relation to the type of sexual deviation.

It is obvious that reliable recidivism rates are of great assistance to a court which is required to pass sentence in the case of an individual offender. For example, the information compiled by the clinic indicates that an elderly pedophile rarely, if ever, repeats his offense. This means that it is seldom necessary to sentence an elderly pedophile to imprisonment. A survey of sexual offenders in penal institutions indicates that the courts in Ontario seldom sentence such an offender to imprisonment.

"Pedophilia" may be defined as the expressed desire for immature sexual gratification with a prepubertal child. Not all sexual acts committed by adults with children can be considered pedophilic. Children may be involved in other deviant acts as exhibitionism or in a small number of cases in acts in which coitus is the final sexual aim. The majority of sexual offenses against children, however, consist of those of immature gratification involving fondling, showing, looking, and masturbation. According to the sex of the child, one can distinguish between homosexual pedophilia and heterosexual pedophilia. In only a small number of cases will a sexual act be committed with both sexes. These offenders usually tend toward a polymorphous sexuality.

The pedophilic offenders are all men. Pedophilic offenders fall into three age groupings: adolescence, the middle to late thirties, and the late fifties. The first group shows a lag in their psychosexual maturation. The second group is characterized by a breakdown of adjustment to the adult world, mainly in terms of family relationships; and the third group is characterized by loneliness and impotence.

Significant differences occur between the heterosexual and homosexual pedophile in terms of follow-up. The chances for a homosexual pedophile to repeat the offense is about twice as high as for a heterosexual pedophile.

Further differences occur between first offenders and those who have committed more than one offense. The findings in the clinic show a progression from 10 percent for first offenders, to 22 percent with more than one previous sexual offense, to 33 percent for those who had previous sexual and nonsexual offenses. In heterosexual pedophilia the reconviction rate for first offenders lies between 5 and 8 percent, with the adolescent and middle-aged offender on the higher side and the senescent group on the lower side. For those with more than one sexual offense, the expectation of a subsequent sexual offense would lie around 20 percent; and for those who had previous sexual and nonsexual offenses, around 30 percent. In homosexual pedophilia the best estimates would be twice those percentages.

Personal follow-up interview of treated cases supported the documentary data derived from criminal records. Heterosexual pedophiles showed gains in almost all psychological and social areas investigated, whereas more limited gains had been made by homosexual pedophiles. It has to be considered that the homosexual pedophile, as a double deviant, is in a more difficult position. His deviation is usually more ego-syntonic than that of the heterosexual pedophile, whose acts often show strong situational components. This is borne out by the circumstances of the offense and the choice of victim. Heterosexual pedophilic offenses tend to occur in the closer environment of the offender and victim, with the victim being known to the offender in the majority of cases. This is somewhat less the case in homosexual pedophilic offenses, which also tend to have a stronger element of planning.

Heterosexual pedophilic offenses tend, therefore, to be of an incidental nature and a random court sample should contain no more than 10 percent recidivists. The number of chronic offenders is small. There is a further decrease of recidivism by age, which means that the chances of repeating the offense are exceedingly small for a senescent pedophilic first offender.

Homosexual pedophilic offenders, although tending more toward chronicity than heterosexual ones, still show a relatively good recovery rate, especially after the first offense, when about 80 percent can be expected not to repeat the offense.

The incidence of pedophilia in the cases attending the forensic clinic is shown in Table VI. This table covers the period from

TABLE VI. *Forensic Clinic, Toronto Psychiatric Hospital, incidence of pedophilia, May 1, 1956 to April 30, 1962*

Offense	Court referral	Noncourt referral	Total	Percentage of total
Exhibitionism	119	48	167	24.8
Pedophilia	98	52	150	22.2
Homosexuality	75	190	265	39.3
Incest	10	11	21	3.1
Voyeurism	9	11	20	3.0
Transvestism	6	13	19	2.8
Other	12	20	32	4.8
Total	329	345	674	100.0

May 1, 1956 to April 30, 1962. During this period 1414 new patients were examined in the clinic. Of these, 674, or 47.7 percent, were sex offenders. Table VI shows the numbers and percentages of the types of sexual deviation found in the 674 sex offenders.

The clinic is able to provide a wide range of treatment facilities, including individual psychotherapy, reconditioning techniques, and group therapy. Location of the clinic in a hospital enables the staff of the clinic to utilize all of the facilities for physical investigation which are contained in a modern hospital.

Something of a more general nature might be said about the function of forensic services for the courts. It was pointed out at the beginning of this article that there is a decline in the use of psychiatric services for the purpose of formulating an opinion about the criminal responsibility of an accused person and there has been a corresponding increase in the use of these services in relation to sentence. In Toronto the selection of the cases which are referred to either the inpatient forensic service or the outpatient forensic clinic is made by the trial judge or magistrate. There is usually no preceding medical or psychiatric examination. The experience of the staff of the Toronto Psychiatric Hospital indicates that a judge or magistrate is competent to make this selection without medical assistance, and it is rare that a case is referred for mental examination without justification. A classification follows of the cases in which psychiatric examination is of particular value.

Unexplained Assaults

In this type of case, particularly where a husband has assaulted his wife, there is frequently an underlying mental disorder which can usually be determined by clinical investigation.

Impulsive Acts of Violence

This refers to the kind of case where the evidence shows some act of violence for which there appears no obvious explanation. These cases occur from time to time in every magistrate's court. The referral of such a person to a psychiatric clinic will usually reveal symptoms of a mental illness which is the proximate cause of the antisocial conduct. In one case a woman was employed in the kitchen of a general hospital. She stabbed the woman working next to her. There was no preceding argument or evidence of hostility. Clinical examination showed that the woman was suffering from a schizophrenic illness of several months duration which had not been recognized by her friends or associates. She was treated in a mental hospital as an alternative to imprisonment. In another case a young man seized a policeman's revolver and ran away with it. There was no preceding altercation or explanation for his act. He was referred to the forensic service where it was found that he was in the early stages of a psychotic illness.

Theft

There are some cases of theft in which the act seems to be committed without any advantage to the offender. Psychiatric examination is usually of value in such cases. For example, a man stole articles over a period of one year with a total value of more than $2,500. He did not sell any of the articles or make any use of them. He was a good worker, supporting his wife and two young children. He had no previous criminal record. He was referred for examination and it was found that he was subject to episodes of compulsive stealing which he could not control. He had difficulty in controlling his compulsive thefts even while he was on bail awaiting trial. He showed other neurotic manifestations including claustrophobia and compulsive counting. It is obvious that the criminal conduct in this case is the product of a neurotic illness for which the offender requires treatment. Other examples are men who are referred to the clinic, charged with theft, having stolen articles of women's clothing. There is an underlying sexual deviation in these cases. For example, on investigation some of them have turned out to be transvestites.

Attempted Suicide

It is considered that all these cases should receive psychiatric examination; most of them are depressed persons who need treatment.

Amnesia

In these cases the accused alleges a loss of memory for a period of time during which the offense is committed. Some of them are malingerers but some of them have a genuine loss of memory. Clinical investigation will usually distinguish the amnesia cases from the malingerers. It is usually possible to determine the cause of the amnesia, such as, for example, alcohol, hysteria, epilepsy, trauma. Where necessary, special methods of investigation are used, including lie detection tests and narcoanalysis.

Arson

In some cases of arson the evidence indicates that the accused caused a fire without any hope of financial gain or other obvious motivation. Some of the offenders are mentally defective. In other cases there is an emotional illness and there may be a sexual deviation involved.

Sex Offenders

Sex offenders are a particularly suitable group for psychiatric diagnosis and treatment as an alternative to imprisonment. The recidivism rate is very low in the case of sex offenders as compared with other crimes. There is high incidence of neurotic disorder in these cases and this is no doubt one of the reasons why they respond favorably to psychiatric treatment. On the other hand, this group does include some very dangerous people. The ongoing researches in the Forensic Clinic should assist in the development of criteria for the selection of the offenders who can be treated as an alternative to imprisonment without undue risk to the community.

Crimes Without Motivation

In addition to the above groups there are cases where, regardless of the charge, the conduct of the accused was obviously silly and childish, being the result of a mental disorder or gross mental defect.

SUMMARY

A decline in the number of cases in which insanity is pleaded as a defense in a criminal trial in Canada is described. Concomitantly, there has been a rise in the number of cases in which psychiatric evidence is used in relation to the sentence of a person convicted of a crime.

The facilities at the Toronto Psychiatric Hospital for the examination and treatment of adult offenders are explained. Some of the researches are discussed in detail, particularly the attempt to formulate prediction tables for the use of courts in sentencing. The topic of pedophilia is selected as a specific illustration of the use of psychiatric facilities by the courts. A classification is made of the types of offenses in which psychiatric examination is of particular value.

Functioning of the Superego in Delinquents

NOËL MAILLOUX

It is commonplace among law-abiding citizens to describe the habitual delinquent as a ruthless rebel, whose hardened conscience seems almost impervious to morality and unembarrassed by guilt and remorse. Even the more sophisticated representatives of the law still hold this view, although they are making a decisive move in the right direction in recognizing that the legal responsibility of the so-called "psychopath" may be just as questionable as that of the psychotic offender. Such a generally accepted notion will seem hard to challenge. It appears strongly substantiated by the everyday observation of the thousands of recidivists, who have never been deterred from their mischievous designs even by the most severe punishments and constitute the chronic population of our penitentiaries. It may also be considered as fully warranted by the long-lived descriptive classifications proposed by classic sociology and psychiatry.

However, after conducting weekly group therapy sessions with

This investigation is part of a more comprehensive study of the "process of socialization," now being conducted by the *Centre de Recherches en Relations Humaines* and supported by a grant from the Aquinas Fund. Basic research in the field of juvenile delinquency is an essential part of this program. It has been made possible since the senior investigator received the first career research fellowship offered by the National Research Fund of the Canadian Mental Health Association. Acknowledgment is also gratefully extended to Mr. Gilles Gendreau, Director of Boscoville, and to all the educators of this most progressive institution for their enthusiastic collaboration throughout the investigation.

five groups of habitual delinquents for over five years, a surprisingly different picture is emerging from the mass of observational material as it is closely scrutinized. This long-term investigation has been carried out at Boscoville in the Province of Quebec, a residential reeducation center, situated near Montreal, Canada. Each group involved in this research comprised an average of twelve boys, from 17 to 20 years old, living together in separate quarters under the supervision of two specialized educators. As they come in contact with each other only at mealtime or in competitive sports, such groups tend to develop a definite identity of their own. All the boys are committed by the court, after a number of serious offenses, for a period of two years. Newcomers replace those who leave but at a rather slow rate and only when they can be absorbed by the group without considerably affecting the constellation of forces in action at a given stage of the reeducation process. In fact, their admission into one of these treatment groups takes place only after an initial phase of adaptation, lasting approximately twelve weeks, has been completed in the observation center. Of course, their arrival brings temporary reinforcement to those who remain entrenched in their delinquent attitudes; but, at the same time, it necessitates the taking of a firm stand on the part of those who have become openly amenable to socializing influences. Experience has shown that such tension provides an indispensable prop for deep-reaching therapeutic endeavors, since all attempts at influencing more homogeneous control groups proved to be far more laborious and yielded less conclusive results.

At the present stage, with the help of experienced and highly trained educators, the whole program has been so structured as to make use of all the daily activities for the aims of reeducation and has reached a degree of efficiency one would not have dreamed of in the early years of the institution's life. A boy who is introduced into any group irresistibly feels the impact of a therapeutic milieu which may tolerate a fair amount of delinquent acting out but not without making him aware of it and soon rendering it rather unrewarding. Thus, the complacent display of the street corner gang's symbols, i.e., bad language, boisterous grappling, unkempt hair, weird attire, etc., once so difficult to eradicate, can barely be observed anymore in our groups. With hardly any explicit intervention on our part, many an initial resistance wanes readily, as relatively socialized patterns of conduct and attitudes are directly transmitted to the new recruits by the few admired pals whose reeducation is well under way. Of course, as long as the latter are there, a number of those who display such drastic changes in their external behavior will continue to pretend that their basic intent has not been altered in the least. Secretly, however, they prepare to follow in their footsteps and they proudly assume, in their turn, the role of models as soon as their idealized predecessors leave.

Several years of intensive therapeutic work are required before this kind of self-perpetuating reeducation process will permit *a whole group* to develop such a strong collective ego involvement, so to speak, that ever deeper probing into the underlying dynamics of delinquent behavior will become possible. Thus, astonishing insights are attained that lead to a progressive elucidation of the functioning and crystallizing of the typical delinquent superego. The following interpretations, albeit sketchy and provisional, will allow a more penetrating comprehension of some of the crucial distortions that, in the habitual delinquent, transform the superego into an irreconcilable protagonist of moral conscience.

DELINQUENTS ARE NOT AMORAL HUMAN BEINGS

As is well known, the dynamism which constitutes the mainspring of our moral life draws on *two psychic instances* of basically different orders: the superego and the conscience. Where there is a successful integration, these two instances are so well articulated and blended that they are finally seen as the unique, efficacious principle of *human* action. It is in this same way that empirical observation and logical thought are integrated in the scientist, and creative imagination and esthetic intuition in the artist. On the other hand, in certain cases, this normal integration does not come about. It can be seen at once that the more or less erratic interferences of a nonsyntonic superego render the conscience decidedly ineffective in the exercise of its essential functions, i.e., lucid moral judgment, efficacious dictates, and sanction amounting to uncompromising self-approval or remorse. This discovery of contemporary psychology goes back several years (1, 6), and in certain realms of psychopathology, many investigators have grasped the extent of its implications and drawn really illuminating applications from it. The time has come to do likewise in clinical criminology, if we wish once and for all to dispel the confusion in which so many attempts at interpretation of delinquent behavior are still bogged down.

First of all, many fruitless disputes, which for too long have divided jurists and psychologists, could have been avoided, if only they had taken the trouble to discover a fact evident to anyone who has had occasion to observe delinquents closely; namely, that like the majority of the average citizens around them, most delinquents are equipped with a conscience capable of making value judgments with a minimum of discernment. The majority, in fact, whatever have been their misdeeds and from whatever environment they come, are perfectly capable of distinguishing good from evil and recognize the illegality of the activities in which they are involved. This, however, is not the problem. Moreover, if we make an effort to understand fully those who are forced into recidivism by a compulsion to repeat actions censured by their conscience, we very soon become aware that in such individuals unconscious forces nullify the power of moral judgment and prevent it from exerting a normal influence on conduct. Like the neurotic, as will be explained later, the delinquent is vaguely aware that he is the plaything of an elusive fatality and comes to the point where he feels that he is at the mercy of a determinism from which he very soon loses all hope of escaping.

There are some who have clearly grasped the pernicious role surreptitiously played by the superego in the triggering off and persistence of antisocial behavior. Even these persons, however, have consistently looked upon the delinquent as an individual devoid of authentic moral conscience and consequently have totally disregarded the share which should fittingly be attributed to it in the work of reeducation. It is well known that in the treatment of neurotics, the ego, in spite of its temporary helplessness, remains an indispensable prop, due to the fact that it permits the maintenance of a contact, however tenuous, with reality. Now, it would seem to be fitting to assign an analogous role to moral conscience in the treatment of delinquency. Similarly, although reduced to helplessness for the time being, it does not cease to keep alive in the delinquent's mind an image of the unimpeachable values which will of necessity confront the aberrant norms suggested by an insidiously deformed superego. Even if this does nothing to help the delinquent foster indispensable moral inhibitions, he is never completely deaf to the rational dictates of his conscience. A profound despair prevents him from believing that he can ever, through his own resources, succeed in making them the rule of his conduct. Nevertheless, it is there that he will discover solid support for his effort at reeducation, when he has the feeling that he is finally among people who have the necessary competence to understand, guide, and support him.

A CRUCIAL ISSUE IN THE STUDY
OF HABITUAL DELINQUENCY

Starting with such a statement of the problem, the need will be felt to go beyond certain classifications, based on criteria which are much too descriptive and immediately seem artificial. This is because they incite us to see in the delinquent an individual who is partially or totally devoid of an authentic moral sense and incapable of being affected by the reactions it spontaneously triggers off. To mention only those classifications which have immediate implications for us, we find it difficult to accept those which are content to distinguish: between delinquents, who, in spite of all their transgressions, never experience the dawning of any feeling of guilt and those who, on the other hand, act under the sway of guilt feelings derived from an unresolved oedipal conflict (2); and between individual and sociologic or gang delinquents, in whom the superego shows functional lacunae, resulting from a harmful indulgence on the part of the parents or from the influence of a perverse subculture which has originally contaminated their whole environment (4). Instead of dwelling on categorizations which tend to evade rather than resolve the difficulty, it is essential to remember that habitual delinquency is a symptomatic manifestation where the functioning of the superego, which thwarts rather than promotes the lucid assertion of conscience, must be subjected to a thorough analysis. This is the problem we intend to deal with here with the aid of the explicit and repeated verbalizations, which we have been able to collect and interpret in depth in the course of our interviews with our five groups of boys from Boscoville. However daring the following formulation may appear in the present stage of our research, it contains at least a valid and interesting hypothesis.

THE STUMBLING BLOCK
OF REEDUCATION

First of all, we shall start with a universally accepted fact: the habitual delinquent is deeply rooted in a narcissistic attitude, which immediately prevents him from becoming attached to anyone in a lasting, friendly, and confident way. This makes him almost impermeable to all educational influences and obliges us, if we wish to have an effect on him, to perfect highly specialized treatment techniques. But what is more serious is that such an attitude entrenches the delinquent in a state of immaturity, preventing him from realizing that, as a human being, he has an inalienable and transcendant value, which remains intact despite his behavioral aberrations. On the other hand, the delinquent feels that his ego and his actions are identical, the former of necessity being valorized or devalorized by the latter. Conscious of his numerous misdeeds, he thus sees himself as the very incarnation of badness or, if we wish, as wicked by nature. Encouraged by all those who have incessantly seen him, in anticipation, as the black sheep who would one day reveal himself (5), he is led to consider his behavior as an inborn trait, in no way amenable to correction. We will consider in more detail the main implications for treatment of the pathological crystallization of such an ignominious self-perception, too often compensated through a delusional affectation of grandiose ideas and deeds.

SOME MANIFESTATIONS OF
DEVASTATING GUILT FEELINGS

It is now necessary to go a step further and show how the delinquent is hopelessly doomed to become the victim of an implacable superego, which, even before he has committed a seriously reprehensible act, condemns him to feel under the spell of immeasurable and irreversible guilt because it is inherent in the very substance of his being. As he feels that his worth consists entirely in *what he is doing*, rather than in *what he is* as a human being, he is bound to see in any of his subsequent offenses only new evidence of his innate wickedness. This is so true that even after two years of treatment, our young delinquents are practically unanimous in asserting that they cannot walk down the street without having the impression that all the passersby recognize them by their appearance and bearing. They are under the sway of magical thought to such an extent that they barely hesitate to add, in reference to myself, that even if it should happen that they went out in my clerical garb, it would not be long before they were recognized.

Even when they have not committed any misdemeanor for a long time, they feel a distrust and a suspicion weighing on them. They complain bitterly about the inescapable perspective of remaining the lifelong victims of an unfair discrimination, which seems real to them because they still unconsciously consider these supposed attitudes of distrust and suspicion sufficiently justified to project them onto others. This diffuse feeling of guilt continues to haunt them for a long time to such an extent that it is with great difficulty that they lose the conviction of being always closely watched. Similarly, they can hardly resist an almost instinctive need to run away, if by chance they see a policeman appear. This conviction also prevents them from feeling at ease except in the company of "old pals," who have been rehabilitated at the same time as themselves; and likewise makes them hesitant to cross the threshold of a recreation hall or a department store.

If at such an advanced stage in treatment the superego can still mobilize such primitive guilt and suggest such a deformed interpretation of social reality, what must be expected in the initial stage? This will be understood without too much difficulty if an effort is made to explicate and reveal the logical sequence of the verbalizations of a group of boys who see themselves as born thieves. For them, as for everybody, property is a natural need. A spontaneous inclination impels them to appropriate everything around them which can ensure the satisfaction of their desires as well as their subsistence. Unfortunately, scarcely has their ego endorsed the identity of the born thief, than the tranquil possession of an object becomes impossible for them, no matter how it has been acquired. Even if they have in their pockets a few dollars honestly earned, they do not have the impression that it really belongs to them. For them, it is just as if they had stolen it from someone else and they are sure that they would be accused of this at once if it were discovered that they were in possession of this sum of money. It is not surprising, therefore, that they feel an irresistible urge to part with it as soon as possible, as they consistently do with all stolen money, being eager to benefit by it before it is taken from them, or squandering it extravagantly to obviate the risk of being caught with it. Incapable of quietly enjoying what is theirs, they feel frustrated and wronged in relation to those people who have possessions.

A violent, blind jealousy incites them to take vengeance on such people by appropriating their goods by ruse or violence. In their opinion, "all wealthy people are nothing but successful racketeers, who, contrary to themselves, were able to get away with the most dishonest deals, just because they enjoyed protection in high places." If it so happens that, after breaking and entering a dwelling, they do not find what they had hoped for, the idea readily comes to them to indulge in acts of vandalism, leaving the place in an indescribable state. By virtue of a paradoxical morality, with which the study of the unconscious has made us familiar, they *feel excused* from robbing others of what they themselves could not possess without *feeling guilty*.

Under cover of a repression, which keeps guilt feelings in check, they will hasten to give free reign to their impulses, pending their reappearance in a rather unexpected form, for example, the desire to be caught by the police and sent to prison. Indeed, the time comes when the satisfaction following a particularly successful *coup* and the thrill or "kick" of a particularly satisfying revengeful act is replaced by the agonizing fear of no longer being able to stop or of being carried away too far by their perverse nature. Then the conviction thrusts itself upon them: that is enough of that for the time being, the time has come to wipe all this out. Thus they have to be imprisoned at any price. To bring this about, the delinquent scarcely hesitates to multiply more and more dangerous misdemeanors, which often give the impression of barefaced boldness and stir up against him a threatening indignation. He hopes in this way that he will finally be discovered, that his frenzied aggression will be cut short, and that he will be protected against himself. Being unable all the same to simply give himself up to the police, everywhere he goes he leaves clues which are almost tantamount to writing his name on the walls; while another roams about openly with his burglar tools under his arm. When finally caught and subjected to a harassing examination, many will readily admit that they are guilty of *all* the misdemeanors of which they are suspected, since they are no longer able to say for sure whether or not they really are.

Nevertheless, often a relatively short period of imprisonment will be enough for the process of repression to do its work so that this overwhelming guilt feeling becomes blurred to the point of becoming imperceptible. As soon as he has the feeling of having paid his debt, a kind of narcissistic delusion—which, incidentally, is very contagious—quickly develops in the delinquent. This incites him to recount with much exaggeration his real or imaginary exploits to his friends who, although they do not believe such boasting, are happy to share his morbid elation. It is from these fantasies that the delinquent, forced to face once again the fearful certainty of relapsing into his past mistakes and reliving the pangs of depressing guilt

feelings, carefully elaborates a plan for the "perfect crime," which
will allow him to pursue his career without ever being caught again.
It will be readily understood that if there is no therapeutic intervention to help him regain contact with reality, such a prisoner becomes a source of particularly virulent contamination to younger
and less experienced inmates, pending a relapse into recidivism as
soon as he is released.

In order to complete this dynamic interpretation of the danger-
ously pathological functioning of the delinquent's superego, it
would be interesting to have recourse to the numerous observations
collected in the course of treatment. Already, the modifications
which mark the principal phases of reeducation lead us to see in a
new light a very complex dynamic functioning which we have at
least tried to outline here. The more we understand the many
nuances involved, the nearer we will be to a complete understanding
of the problem. To formulate them clearly, we hope to be able to
build on a more solid foundation. However fragmentary the notions
discussed previously may be, they suggest, for the work of reeducation, certain points of reference which justify exceptionally
stimulating hopes.

INITIAL APPROACH TO STUDY
OF ABERRANT SUPEREGO FUNCTIONING

In a recent study (5), a particular endeavor was made to highlight
the determining influence exerted on a child's psychosocial evolution
by the anticipatory picture that his parents form of his future
identity. The conflict stemming from their too often explicit fore-
boding of the humiliating prospect of being responsible for having
brought a black sheep into the world, seems to us in the case of
young recidivists to be the nucleus around which supervenes the
crystallization of their delinquent attitude. Moreover, such an outcome seems to take on as inevitable a character as classic neuroses,
which result from an unsolved oedipal conflict and are constantly
exacerbated by the sexual immaturity of parents whose conjugal
life leaves a great deal to be desired. Naturally, from the very

beginning of our research, numerous observations led us to conclude that parents usually play a determining role in the etiology of habitual delinquency, although this only rarely occurs in a fully conscious manner, implying direct responsibility on their part. This assumption so readily became a certainty that it seemed pointless to dwell at length on the consideration of it. It was for this reason that we preferred to concentrate on the task of delineating the precise modality assumed by certain attitudes, which we knew were liable to exert such an insidious influence on children still in the initial period of their development.

Here, however, we were in for a rather disagreeable surprise. We began to realize more and more how, under the influence of the spell produced by a *negative identification,* the child feels compelled to do the things which his parents, with unfortunate insistence, constantly censure, rather than comply with their reasonable requests. Thus, we could entertain the hope of finding a more expeditious means of rectifying the deviation, as baneful as it is irresistible, which turns the process of socialization in a pathological direction and marks the genesis of a delinquent career. On the other hand, since we were dealing with boys from 17 to 20 years of age, who could be expected to cope adequately on their own in the future, the problem of modifying the existing parental attitudes remained, for all practical purposes, outside of our consideration. We felt that it was not worthwhile to persist, at the cost of a prolonged effort, in trying to ameliorate a relationship almost desperately deformed by hostility and misunderstanding, since it was destined, at the end of the process of reeducation, to play no future role. This shows that we were still very far from suspecting that the principal stages of the process of alienation, whereby the delinquent is gradually led to perceive himself as a stranger and an outcast in the very society in which he must live, were merely the aggravated repetitions of this early relationship, the deviant imprint of which would inevitably mark all subsequent relationships. Faced with the formidable implications of this exposure of the mechanism of *repetition compulsion,* a total and thorough reeducation seemed an undertaking of discouraging complexity. Indeed, to put an end to the constant aggravation of delinquent tendencies, which assumed an increasingly manifest symptomatic character, it appeared essential to reach beyond our subjects, to parents solidly anchored in their evasive attitudes.

This problem is not yet resolved. Nevertheless, a clearer perception of the personal evolution which results in a state of irreversible "dissocialization," does allow us to have some idea of certain approaches which are essential for undertaking the work of efficacious reeducation. We propose, therefore, to show successively:

1. How, as a result of repetition compulsion, the preconceived portrait of the future malefactor, which the child assumes as he discerns it through the forebodings of his parents, occasions an increasingly accentuated aberration of his psychosocial development.

2. How a reeducation, which aims at the resocialization of the habitual delinquent, must traverse certain well-defined stages in order to arrive at the root of the symptomatic behavior and ensure a permanent rehabilitation.

THE ROAD TO "DISSOCIALIZATION"

Like the delinquent, the neurotic tends to live more and more on the fringe of society. For the latter, however, it is rather a question of a timid, anxious retreat from society, brought about by an inability to respond adequately to its demands and expectations. The delinquent, on the other hand, begins by feeling driven to keep to his own kind, expecting to see himself irresistibly forced into a way of life which separates him more and more from society and where his deviations will sooner or later place him in conflict with society.

Thus, we should not be surprised that the conviction develops and persists in him that he is a kind of outcast or monster, inevitably destined to be excluded from society. Seeing his misdeeds as nothing other than the manifestation of his perverse nature, he judges himself more severely than his immediate entourage would dare to do. Dominated as he is by innate evil inclinations, he can only be expected to relapse continually and it is a waste of time to try to help him to reform. Such is the attitude in which he is solidly anchored, although in a barely conscious way, at the moment when he leaves the family milieu to go to school. It should be remembered that this attitude is dictated to him by a negative identification, inevitably forced upon him by the suspicions, charges, and forebodings of those who are responsible for his upbringing. Until now, however, in spite of everything, it is often just a question of a "difficult child," who could be rescued relatively easily from a confused impasse by a skillful intervention.

Unfortunately, this intervention is more rare than one imagines. We tend to forget that once this agonizing representation of his future takes root in the interior dynamism of the child, it quickly succeeds in subjugating all his behavior to this obscure *compulsion to repeat*, the power of which Freud described as a "demonic" force (3). In every milieu where he henceforth seeks admittance, without knowing exactly why, he will come up against the same hostile mistrust. Thus will be stifled his last hopes of pulling himself together, by finally finding somewhere a favorable welcome and a glimmer of encouragement. It is as if an ill-fated destiny weighed upon him, continually barring him from access to the society of honest men. It is thus that he is drawn into the fatal rut of hopeless recidivism. The following brief description, reproducing as faithfully as possible the series of actual experiences of the young men with whom we work, will suffice to show how this result finally appears as the only possible means of escape from despair.

If we go back to that moment when the budding delinquent goes to school for the first time, we must realize that he crosses the threshold profoundly marked by the reprobation of which he has been the victim in his family milieu. In mixing with so many new companions, with whom he would like to be friends, he is readily recognized as the "black sheep" by his first pranks which are not long in appearing. Accustomed to being considered as incapable of doing anything well, he will not even take the trouble to try to learn as the others do. Soon, his continual failures will cause him to be classified among the poor students. Then, whenever there is mention of some misdemeanor—probably petty theft—he will be thought of immediately. Once again, he will have to face the suspicions, the humiliating interrogations, the condemnations, and the threats, the implications of which he grasps only too well. As the punishments are multiplied, he will be forced to protect himself against the terror which threatens to overwhelm him by putting up a show of harsh imperturbability. In no time at all, he will be relegated to the back row of the classroom among the neglected pupils from whom little is expected, because they have been labelled once and for all as "incorrigible characters" and "future jailbirds." From that time on, the child, to whom the experience of inescapable condemnation has suggested the impression of his being at the mercy of his impulses, learns to think of himself as a being deprived of all capacities, a prey to a host of perverse inclinations that even the most competent educators feel incapable of helping the child to master. In addition, he is doomed to universal contempt and to the most severe punishments. There is but one step from there to the upsurge of feelings of hatred and revolt which lead him to become callous and to deal the first blow to an aggressor, who has already all the weapons on his side. This step will be taken quickly and will prove decisive. For the first time, repetition compulsion will have done its work .

At this stage, however, the offenses are ordinarily of an occasional and not too alarming nature. The adolescent still entertains a vague hope of finding in the near future, in the anonymous surroundings of work, a liberation from the troublesome demands of school and likewise an opportunity to make the most of himself, while at the same time assuring himself of the long-awaited remuneration, amply sufficient to satisfy all his desires. However, when the moment arrives to seek admittance into the adult world, he quickly realizes that this means becoming involved in intense, continual competition. He finds himself completely devoid of even the most rudimentary means to cope with such competition. If he dares to approach an employer, he immediately realizes after the first few questions, that he is clearly unprepared to take on a man's job and what is even more distressing, that he will perhaps never be capable of doing so. He is offered only the most menial, monotonous, and temporary tasks, which would barely ensure his subsistence and would draw the attention of his acquaintances to his inadequacies. In addition, unskilled and inexperienced as he is, he is readily exposed to contempt, reprimands, and threats of being fired. Thus, he either gives up almost immediately after a few half-hearted attempts or he finds a way to be dismissed once and for all, by being negligent, by quarreling with a supervisor, or by indulging in dishonest practices which will soon be discovered.

The proof is self-evident: even if he so desired, he could accomplish nothing worthwhile and far from being able to satisfy his grandiose whims, he would barely be able to earn enough to satisfy his most elementary needs. It is at this juncture that he is most likely to take refuge for good in the welcoming atmosphere of a delinquent gang. Relying on the experience and suggestions of a few companions, he will soon find enough courage in their company to risk his first major offenses. Once again, repetition compulsion has made him perform all the necessary actions to bring upon himself in the world of work a degrading ostracism which would have condemned him to destitution if it had not authorized him in his own eyes to rise up against those who possess the goods of this world and take away their possessions by ruse or violence. Yesterday's incorrigible rebel has no other alternative than to vegetate or become a professional thief.

But at the very moment when the delinquent adolescent is trying to consolidate his acceptance in a gang, he is usually preoccupied with affirming his virility as soon as possible. To do this, he cannot have recourse to scholastic success, however modest it may be, and to a perspective of the future, giving him access to a role important enough to earn him the consideration of those who count in his eyes. Likewise, he knows that for him there could be no question of getting married, for the very good reason that no serious-minded, respectable girl would dare introduce him to her family as a suitable match. Besides, in relation to her, he would feel too timid and inadequate to take her out with any constancy. Considering himself defeated in advance, he prefers to turn rather to the kind of girls from whom he expects nothing more than an opportunity for diversion or to use his own words, he decides "to sow his wild oats" giving himself up to dissipation and to intemperance in all its forms. Once again, an obscure repetition compulsion immediately evokes in him, in the presence of those he calls "good girls," the feeling of forever being unworthy of their admiration and love, knowing that they would never even dream of recognizing in him the man they would like to see become the father of their children. He feels a resentment which incites him to heap scorn and abuse on women, in whom he claims constantly to find only infidelity and seduction. As far as he himself is concerned, he does not hesitate to debase himself by indulging in rowdy obscenity. While rarely actually going to the excesses he insinuates, he willingly gives the impression of being shamelessly indecent.

Once started on the path of corruption, how can he ever stop before reaching the end of it? One after the other, his companions fall into the hands of the police, and undergo a trial which makes them the talk of the town, following which they serve time in prison. Seeing himself somewhere between such companions and those who make up normal society, he has the impression of having been discounted and feels deprived of any definite identity. If at the time of his first court appearances, the judge is lenient with him and simply sends him home following a short admonition, he is afraid that his companions will think of him as an informer, who knew how to get himself out of a scrape at their expense or at least as a child that no one would take seriously. Therefore, he will take every means at his disposal to ensure official, legal recognition of his status as a delinquent. Following a well-publicized sentence and a prolonged stay in prison, people will know of what stuff he is made. In leading him as far as the threshold of the underworld, repetition compulsion has brought to fruition the ill-fated prophecies formulated by his own family during his childhood: he is now classified among the hardened criminals dedicated to a life of crime.

THREE MAJOR PHASES OF THERAPEUTIC REEDUCATION

Some of my collaborators have highlighted the principal reactions, the obvious resistances, and the latent defense mechanisms which we must be prepared to face at the different moments of a group psychotherapy in which an effort is made to follow, step by step, the evolution through which the young delinquents pass in the course of reeducation. It is now essential to understand better the import of the explicitation of these dynamic factors that my colleagues have outlined.

The first step in this direction consists of indicating the specific manifestation, typical of the deep conflict with which our boys are at grips, at each one of the three essential phases of the process of their resocialization. Moreover, it was in striving to follow the thread of these phenomena and resolve, one by one, the dilemmas they presented that we arrived at the systematic interpretation proposed previously. This interpretation, in its turn, sheds a completely new light on our tentative initial efforts and suggests an increasingly clear, precise orientation. We shall content ourselves for the time being with a schematic presentation, which will take into account only those facts likely to provide us with decisive indications for the efficacious pursuit of our therapeutic effort and for a more penetrating understanding of criminal pathology.

Weakening of the Delinquent Structure

As a result of a precocious negative identification, the young delinquent comes to us unable to distinguish what *he is* from what *he does*. The aberrations of his behavior are perceived by him as so many deficiencies of his nature. For him, to steal is the same as being a thief by nature. This demands the immediate ruling out of any possibility of change and also implies that the consideration of any effort toward reform is absolutely futile. It is, therefore, not surprising that he is immediately prepared to offer a tenacious resistance to any pressure coming from the outside, to any suggestion made by an educator. More important is the fact that an attempt is made to exert an influence on a *whole group* at the same time, which also threatens the interior equilibrium of each of the individuals who constitute it. How can we thus avoid expecting that they will band together at once to present to the aggressor a united front which will not be easy to break down. It is only when this has been achieved, and when the original gang has been fragmented into several subgroups, that an educative influence can be exerted now on individuals. The open resistance of each individual seems to be shaken at the same time as that of the group, because, on his own, no one can hope to withstand this influence which has already succeeded in breaking down the tenacious and powerfully organized opposition of the whole group.

To be sure, they will make numerous attempts to recover themselves and regroup their forces. Even those who admit openly to their bewildered companions that they can foresee the possibility of a radical transformation, and that they propose to collaborate with those who hold out a helping hand, will not hesitate to contradict themselves and take many retrograde steps. Nevertheless, one is aware that a decisive stage has been passed and that the work of reeducation is already underway.

Collective Projection

This is the moment when the group and each person individually begins to understand by means of a lucidity, albeit fleeting, that their behavior will soon take on a new orientation, which in all likelihood will follow its beneficial course. Concomitantly, however, resistance is not long in appearing on another plane, with increased force and a configuration which allows a number of strategic retreats before final capitulation. In fact, our subjects will admit, without too much difficulty, that they are disposed to improve but they begin to raise a number of doubts as to the usefulness of an effort as painful as it is demanding.

Indeed, they affirm more and more forcefully that they can scarcely see the benefits of improved behavior; since when they leave Boscoville, no one will believe that a real change has taken place in them, and they will find themselves in exactly the same impasse as before. It is in this way that they successively retrace the long road traversed under the influence of repetition compulsion.

First of all, they declare that society will continue to treat them as outcasts because their carefully preserved case records will follow them wherever they go and the police will not miss a chance to watch their movements.

Then they will be convinced of the impossibility of ever being able to have a home of their own like other people. No decent girl will be willing to accept them or, on the other hand, if she is friendly, her family will make a point of creating obstacles which will soon put an end to her condescension.

As for the possibility of finding employment which will allow them to earn an honest living, they state plainly that they cannot count on it. Upon learning that they have been at Boscoville, no employer is going to be willing to hire them. Besides, knowing their past history, the employer could hardly refrain from entertaining hurtful suspicions about them and from constantly testing them out. Finally, they will maintain with insistence that, by reason of their limited education, the places frequented by boys of their own age are not for them. Recreation centers, for instance, are not for them because "these places are frequented above all by university students and by young men of a superior class."

One can readily imagine the anxiety precipitated by the necessity of envisaging one after another of these successive adaptations and one can see to what logical acrobatics they will have recourse in order to back up their rationalizations. As one tries to encourage them to get over any one of the stages mentioned previously, all the defense mechanisms which can be used to postpone a reckoning or facilitate an evasion will be profitably used with consummate skill. However, hardly has one succeeded in neutralizing the effects of them and ensured an effective reentry into society, where the apprehensions expressed are really no longer justified, than a new difficulty dawns, which has roots far deeper than all the others.

Return to the Family

The young delinquent whose reeducation is considered a success and who must realize that all the doors of society are henceforth

open to him, comes finally to share with us an anxiety which tor-
ments him more than ever: "How is his family going to receive
him?" This question, which at first seemed of secondary importance, proved finally to be the most fundamental. The reply that
will be given to him is of capital importance for the completion
and consolidation of his reeducation. Indeed, it seems that the
conflict which has given rise to the delinquent pathology cannot
be really solved as long as a favorable outcome to the previous
question has not been found. Indeed, all our young people come
to realize as an inescapable necessity the need to make their
peace with their parents, and to know that they are finally accepted
in the family to the same degree as their siblings, and to be aware
that there is also the sincere conviction that a total reforma-
tion has taken place in them. The majority wish to return to
the home of their parents in order to be able to see for themselves
that they have truly regained the confidence of their families, who
they feel are the people who know them best. But their families
are those who formerly thrust the weight of so much suspicion
and mistrust upon them, suspicion and mistrust which forced
them to become the black sheep of the family. Are they not, in
fact, right in thinking that if at last they are accorded the confidence within the family so long refused them, they could forth-
with confront the world with a new confidence that nothing
would ever be able to shake again? They know that herein lies
the source of all their later difficulties with society and that all
their other relationships ultimately depend upon this initial
relationship.

Alas, up to the present, we have hardly been able to ascertain
all that this ultimate encounter of the young delinquent with his
parents involves in the way of difficulties and risks. All that we
can affirm is that those who have succeeded, with a minimum of
help on our part, in explaining themselves effectively to their
parents and in regaining their confidence, have barely hesitated
in facing up to the requirements of an adult life. After just a few
weeks at home they have been eager to free themselves from all
dependency. In discovering themselves as full members of their

family, they feel at ease in returning there as welcome visitors; but they feel all the more proud at being independent and self-sufficient. As for the others, whose parents barely accept their advances and avoid a frank, friendly explanation, a deep anxiety continues to grip them and their perseverance remains marked by an uneasiness which probably suggests the existence in them of a conflict which, in importance, is second to none—not even the oedipal conflict.

REFERENCES
1. Alexander, F. *Psychoanalysis of the Total Personality.* New York: Nervous and Mental Disease Publishing Co., 1935.
2. Freud, S. Some Character-Types Met with in Psychoanalytic Work. *Collected Papers* (vol. 5). New York: Basic Books, Inc., 1959.
3. Freud, S. *Beyond the Pleasure Principle* (vol. 18). The Standard Edition, 1920, pp. 21-22.
4. Johnson, A. M. Juvenile Delinquency. In S. Arieti (Ed.), *American Handbook of Psychiatry* (vol. 1). New York: Basic Books, Inc., 1959, chap. 42.
5. Mailloux, N., and Lavallée, C. Genèse et signification de la conduite "antisociale." *La Revue Canadienne de Criminologie* 4:103-111, 1962.
6. Odier, C. *Les Deux Sources Consciente et Inconsciente de la Vie Morale* (2nd ed.). Neuchâtel: Editions de la Baconnière, 1947.

Observations on Psychiatry and the Law in Canada

ROBERT O. JONES

This paper reports some observations made during 1954–1956. During this period I had the opportunity to participate on the Royal Commission appointed by the government of Canada to inquire into the law of insanity as a defense in criminal cases. The commission was chaired by the Honorable J. C. McRuer, Chief Justice of the High Court of Justice of Ontario (7). In the course of these inquiries, the commission travelled from St. John's, Newfoundland, to Victoria, British Columbia. We had the opportunity to hear the views of the best legal and psychiatric minds in this country on the present state of the law, the current difficulties, and suggestions for improvement. The proceedings of the commission with their recommendations have been tabled in the House of Commons and in due course may possibly affect legislation in this country. Be that as it may, many interesting and instructive observations accrued which could not possibly form a part of the formal report. This paper concerns itself with some of these observations which seem to me to be of particular importance to psychiatrists and those in related fields.

NEED FOR BETTER UNDERSTANDING
BETWEEN PROFESSIONAL GROUPS

One of the strongest impressions gained was an awareness of the ignorance of lawyers concerning psychiatry and of psychiatrists concerning the law. Even members of the respective professions that were interested in the attitudes of the other showed frequently they did not really understand the other profession. This misunderstanding was highlighted rather amusingly when one distinguished member of the Canadian Bar testified that all criminals should be examined by a board of psychoanalysts before they came to trial. Fearing that this might slow the course of justice even more than at the present, I respectfully inquired if the lawyer would change his testimony to a board of psychiatrists rather than psychoanalysts. He looked at me with an all-forgiving pity in his eyes and replied: "I don't care if they are men or women."

The legal profession seemed to be divided evenly into those who had no knowledge or regard for psychiatry and those who naively expected the psychiatrist to cure the psychopath in ten easy lessons. The first group were represented very largely by aging magistrates, some of whom vigorously proclaimed that they had presided over a busy court for 20 years and never had a psychiatric patient before them. The second group sentenced practically every offender to psychiatric examination and treatment, secure in the belief that the probing of mischief in the unconscious would quickly solve all the problems of their clientele.

On the psychiatric side, few psychiatrists appreciated the essential set-up of the courtroom where the model for prosecution and defense more closely resembles the two opponents in a joust than two collaborators in a research laboratory seeking *Truth*. This point is well made by Guttmacher and Weihofen (4) when they say that the present-day criminal trial is not a scientific investigation after truth but an adversary proceeding; that is, it is a fight between adversaries, each of whom is actuated only by a personal desire to win. Zilboorg (11) elaborates on this and suggests that "adversary" is but a euphemism for "enemy." Zilboorg goes on: "The most typical characteristic of the struggle between enemies is that they are not intent on saving anybody [not even the defendant I am tempted to say] but only on winning their own battle or annihilating their adversary." In this atmosphere, each of the adversaries is out to win, for his own personal satisfaction and because his training has instilled in him the idea that success in his profession demands winning this kind of fight. Zilboorg (11) goes further and suggests that the defendant is forgotten and serves only as the focus of the two hates. In his words, "the defendant as a person, as a human being, all too often stands a perfect chance of being forgotten, since he is but a tool in the duel between two narcissisms: defense and persecution."

This attitude is often exceedingly difficult for the doctor to understand. In fact, he is apt to regard it as barbaric and feel that the lawyer should search for the whole truth of the situation and use this understanding as the basis for his handling of the defendant. Here again, I believe there is a fundamental difference between the doctor and the lawyer. The lawyer is indeed anxious to know everything about the accused and the circumstances of the crime. This is not for the purpose of devising an appropriate punishment which the doctor would call "therapy," but rather to ensure that everything is said for or against the accused, so that if he is found guilty his punishment may be determined not by his need but by what the law says is appropriate for the specific crime. Thus, the lawyer will believe that every man who comes to trial (and if I am ever arrested, I certainly want my lawyer to believe this) has the right to the utilization of every fragment of the law to provide the best possible defense for him. Such a defense involves not only the question of guilt but also the mitigating circumstances, the degree of responsibility, and so on. The severity of the sentence will depend upon such questions. The psychiatrist is called then, not as we fondly believe to help determine the truth of the situation but to supply every fact that will favor the viewpoint of one of the lawyers. In the true "joust" situation, the other lawyer will of necessity do his best to secure the facts on the other side and, if it seems advantageous, present another expert who may well be more adept at discovering the facts wanted by this particular lawyer.

This situation leads to the so-called "battle of the experts." My observations lead me to believe that it is nearly always necessary since the defense lawyer and the prosecution will want to stress different facts. It has been my experience in the courts of Canada that two psychiatrists will nearly always agree on their fundamental opinion about the accused. When their knowledge is tapped by opposing lawyers, however, their stories appear to be different. This is similar to what happens when the psychiatrist has to make a clinical diagnosis. Most of the time we are able to agree on such fundamentals as what is basically wrong with the patient and how he should be handled. Despite this, when it comes to selecting the facts to be stressed in the choice of a particular diagnostic label, there is frequently considerable disagreement.

Zilboorg (11) has made some interesting comments on the difference between the psychology of the doctor and that of the lawyer. He points out that the lawyer's training is case-centered, while the doctor's training is patient-centered. The lawyer cannot be expected to put himself in his client's position or to experience the same behavior for which the client is being tried. The doctor, on the other hand, deals with the people whom he has been taught to see, and feel for and with, and he knows that he may well find himself with exactly the same illness as his patient. In Zilboorg's words:

> However, the conclusion imposes itself that the lawyer [for our purposes, the criminal lawyer] is taught emotionally, sociologically, and professionally to be estranged from the people who will become his major concern as a judge or prosecutor or defense counsel. By the same token, the conclusion imposes itself that the physician is taught to become emotionally, sociologically, and professionally one with the people in the medical conditions which are to become his chief professional concern.

The doctor then learns to turn his hatred against the illnesses from which patients suffer, not against the patient. The lawyer, on the other hand, is imbued with a hatred of the perpetrator of crime just as much as he is against the crime, and carries a hostility with him even though he may have to put himself in the role of the defender of this particular criminal. It is as if every patient with whom the doctor deals is an aggressive psychopath.

When we deal with this kind of patient, I think we generally have much the same attitude as the lawyer.

My experience in listening to psychiatric testimony across the country made me feel that some of my colleagues who had spent a good part of their professional life in contact with the psychopathic criminal had indeed developed very much the same kind of feelings as many lawyers. I would suggest that the thought could be added to Zilboorg's formulations that the attitudes of both professions are not determined entirely by their early training but are modified by their day-to-day experience. Lawyers are not always tough, demanding vengeance; psychiatrists are not always merciful with the feeling that everyone should be treated and no one should be punished. There are hanging judges, and there are hanging psychiatrists. On a number of occasions, psychiatrists who devoted a good deal of their professional life to the examination of criminals, and who usually appeared for the prosecution in any such trials that happen in a particular geographical area, frequently seemed to have lost their "therapeutic orientation" and have had it replaced by a "punishment orientation."

A number of suggestions were put before the commission that, following the actual establishment of guilt or nonguilt by the jury, the question of the disposal of the prisoner should be turned over to the judge and a panel of experts, or solely to the panel, usually composed of psychiatrists. I would hesitate to leave my fate, were I found guilty of murder, in the hands of some of my professional brethren who have spent 30 years testifying as crown witnesses. Experts can be exceedingly biased. I would believe that justice is more likely to result from the deliberation of 12 good men and true, who, though ignorant, are able to empathize with the man on the dock, than from the deliberations of many of the individuals who would form the majority of a panel of experts.

Insanity as a defense in criminal cases is another area in which psychiatrists are remarkably uninformed and naive regarding the legal position. Many psychiatrists believe that the question before the court is whether or not the prisoner is insane, i.e., psychotic, either at the present moment or at the time the crime was committed. If he is insane at the time of the trial, many psychiatrists would say that he is not fit to stand trial; and if he were insane at the time of committing the crime, they would say that he is not guilty because of insanity. Such is not the case. The question of fitness to stand trial has never been clearly defined, but certainly a man who is clinically psychotic may well stand trial. In broad terms, the criteria here are whether or not the accused can understand the proceedings of the trial and can instruct counsel. An extremely psychotic paranoid, for example, may well understand everything that is going on, indeed may be very alert and may well be able to instruct his counsel; and despite the fact that he is psychotic, he can certainly stand trial. The same paranoid who may have obvious delusions regarding his wife's fidelity may shoot a teller in the course of a bank robbery; and in this case his psychosis is no defense. The law is not primarily concerned with the question of existing psychosis. Indeed, known psychotics have been sentenced and have been hanged. The law's concern is with *responsibility*—Does the patient suffer from mental disease which is so severe that he ought not to be held responsible for his act? Thus, the aim of the law and the psychiatrist through the years has been to determine not if the patient was mentally ill at the time of his offense but rather if his mental illness was of such severity that he was not responsible for his act.

THE DEFENSE OF INSANITY IN CANADA

The previous discussion brings me to one of the most important issues which it was the primary duty of this commission to examine; namely, the rules which should be applied to the determination of responsibility and the way in which these could best be written down for universal application. Another contributor to this volume has outlined the history of this search throughout the years. I shall not repeat this material but only deal with the present Canadian law. Most practicing psychiatrists, and, with due respect, most lawyers and many judges, have not fully appreciated what the Canadian law actually is. Discussants of the Canadian law, while occasionally indicating that there is some slight change in the wording from the English law, still say that we essentially follow the M'Naghten Rule. Actually, the Criminal Code which became Canada's law on the first day of July, 1893, contained a rewording of the test for responsibility of so fundamental a nature that a discussion of the original M'Naghten Rules hardly applies. To quote the Royal Commission report: "The rules laid down by the judges in England in answer to the question submitted to them arising out of the M'Naghten case form a historical background to the Canadian law, but neither the answers propounded nor the jurisprudence founded on them in England constitute the Canadian law" (7).

The basis for this argument lies in the change of wording. The M'Naghten Rule and the English law to this day state that the accused shall be excused from responsibility if he "was labouring under such a defect of reason from disease of the mind as not to know the nature and quality of the act he was doing or if he did know it, that he did not know what he was doing was wrong." In Canada the test for responsibility is phrased "incapable of appreciating the nature and quality of the act." The comment of the commission is: "This is not synonymous with knowing the nature and quality of the physical act." Apparently this change was made deliberately to take into account factors other than cognitive. The commission says:

Under the Canadian statute law, a disease of the mind that renders the accused person incapable of an appreciation of the nature and quality of the act must necessarily involve more than mere knowledge that the act is being committed; there must be an appreciation of the factors involved in the act and the mental capacity to measure and foresee the consequences of the violent conduct (7).

As an example of the difference, the testimony of Sir David Henderson, appearing before the English Royal Commission on Capital Punishment, is quoted:

In my opinion, there are many different forms of mental disorder, all of which equally should exonerate a person from a charge of criminal conduct; for example, melancholia, schizophrenia, paranoid states, general paralysis, senile dementia, epilepsy with insanity, and many others. In many of the above cases the individual's mind is sufficiently clear to know what he is doing, but at the same time the true significance of his conduct is not appreciated either in relation to himself or others.

The commission concludes: "The word 'appreciating' not being a word that is synonymous with 'knowing' requires far-reaching legal and medical consideration when discussing Canadian law" (7).

This rewording of the rule from "know" to "appreciate" may well appear to the psychiatrist to be an example of legal quibbling and of little significance. The Royal Commission goes on to examine this point at great length and decides otherwise. They point out that the defining of criminal responsibility is subject to the provisions of the Interpretation Act* which make it obligatory that the law shall receive "a fair, large and liberal construction and interpretation as will best insure the attainment of the object of the Act and of such provision or enactment, according to its true intent, meaning, and spirit."

Many examples have been quoted to show that Canadian courts liberally interpret the law, and the commission reacted violently to the idea that this liberal interpretation was "stretching the law" and felt that it was rather the kind of interpretation that was necessary in Canada to accomplish the intent, meaning, and spirit of the legislation. They suggest (7) that the correct instruction to the Canadian jury is:

If you find a mere preponderance of probability based on the evidence taken as a whole the accused was laboring under natural imbecility or disease of the mind to such an extent as to render him incapable of foreseeing and measuring the consequences of his act or of estimating aright or perceiving the full force of his act, you should find him not guilty on account of insanity; or if on a mere preponderance of probability based on the evidence taken as a whole you come to the conclusion that the accused was laboring under a natural imbecility or disease of the mind to

* *Revised Statutes of Canada,* 1952, Chapter 158, Section 15.

such an extent that he was incapable of knowing that the act was wrong (and by that I do not mean merely legally wrong but wrong in the sense that it was something he ought not to do and for which he would be condemned in the eyes of his fellow men) you should find him not guilty on account of insanity.

That this is not of mere academic concern is supported by the statement in the *Toronto Star*, April 12, 1957, describing the trial of one Peter Woodcock, a 17-year-old boy who had murdered a 4-year-old girl. The judge in his charge to the jury said as follows: "To be insane he must have a disease of the mind that deprives him of the ability to appreciate the nature of his act or that the act was wrong." Mr. Justice Spence went on: "I think the word appreciate is not appreciated in the law. That's my personal opinion."

As a member of this commission, it seemed to me that the interpretation put on Canadian law by my learned legal friends was correct and that with this interpretation most of the problems of psychiatric testimony in our law courts would be solved. However, from personal experience and from a study of a number of Canadian cases, I felt, and in this my colleague, Her Honor Judge Helen Kinnear of the County Court of the County of Haldimand, Ontario, concurred, that the subtleties of the word "appreciate" were not widely appreciated by Canadian courts (as Mr. Justice Spence had pointed out). For this reason, while not disagreeing with the conclusions of the majority of the commission, we felt that justice would be better served if the law in Canada were changed and in a dissenting report we recommended such a change in terms of a modification of the Durham Rule as propounded in the District of Columbia. However, the Canadian law remains as originally written; and it is my belief that since the filing of the McRuer Report, the word "appreciate" has been more generally recognized by the courts and that defenses have been more commonly built around it. I would expect this trend to continue as this point is brought to the attention of lawyers and psychiatrists.

Judge Kinnear and myself also were convinced, after a perusal of the testimony before the commission, that the doctrine of diminished responsibility should be introduced into Canadian law. The problem, I think, is most clearly stated in the case of the mentally retarded individual. At the present moment we are asked to make judgment as to either complete responsibility or no responsibility at all. Who can say at what point this sudden break occurs. This point has been argued in English law for a good many years. Sir James Stephen (8), in his *History of the Criminal Law of England,* wrote that diseases of the brain may:

> . . . cause definite intellectual error and if they do so, their legal effect is that of other innocent mistakes of fact. Far more frequently they affect the will by either destroying altogether or weakening to a greater or lesser extent the power of steady, calm attention to any train of thought and especially to general principles and their relation to particular acts. They may weaken all the mental faculties so as to reduce life to a dream. They may act like a convulsive fit. They may operate as resistible motives to an act known to be wrong. In other words, they may destroy, they may weaken, or they may leave unaffected the power of self-control. The practical inference from this seems to me to be that the law should recognize the various effects of madness. Where madness is proved, it should allow the jury to return any one of three verdicts: guilty; guilty but his power of self-control was diminished by insanity; not guilty on the ground of insanity.

Despite this statement by one of the most eminent of English jurists in 1883 and despite the fact that the principle of diminished responsibility had been tried in Scotland and found to work satisfactorily for a good many years, no change has yet been brought about in Canadian law.

In England, however, in 1957, diminished responsibility was introduced with the thought that a defense would be provided for types and degrees of mental abnormality which would not be accepted as justifying a verdict of guilty but insane. As reported by Nigel Walker (10), in *The Listener* of August 29, 1963, such an opportunity has been achieved. He says: "Impulsive psychopaths, for example, who would have had little chance of establishing insanity within the meaning of the M'Naghten Rules have successfully pleaded diminished responsibility." He goes on to point out that some of the murderers who would have been found guilty but insane before 1957 now use this defense. He says: "These were probably the borderline cases which used to be squeezed past the M'Naghten Rules by the combined efforts of medical witnesses, judges, and juries but which are now being dealt with more openly as cases of diminished responsibility." Walker feels that this new defense in England has allowed many people such as mentioned previously to have the severity of their sentence reduced because of diminished responsibility and that this is particularly so with regard to the type of case that troubles us all; namely, the psychopath. I presume if our dissenting opinion had been accepted, such would be the case in the Canadian courts. At the same time, one wonders just where the psychopath does fit with the wide interpretation of the word "appreciate" as sketched previously.

To summarize, it seems to me that with this use of "appreciate," there is little difficulty in the defense of the individual who is psychotic and whose crime is related to his psychosis. Also, there is little difficulty in the unimportant cases of compulsive behavior of a criminal sort. I am exceedingly interested, however, in the question of the psychopath, which I believe is intellectually the most interesting question in medical-legal psychiatry at the moment. The questions which may be raised in this area deal with whether or not the psychopathic personality is "a disease of the mind" and if it is a disease of the mind, does it prevent a person from "appreciating the nature and quality of his act." It is my feeling that any modern and conscientious psychiatrist will be forced to agree that the psychopath suffers from a disease of the mind. It is not difficult to say that he has no psychosis, neurosis, or organic brain disease, though the latter might be hotly disputed by a number of prominent psychiatrists. In a recent English textbook, *Psychological Medicine,* by Drs. Curran and Partridge (1), I find this statement in their discussion of the etiology of psychopathic personality:

A special peculiarity worthy of note is the occurrence of cerebral dysrhythmia; that is, of abnormal electrical discharges from the brain as recorded by the electroencephalograph. This is mainly

found in the aggressive type of psychopath and according to some
authorities may occur in 65 percent of them as compared with
10 percent in the ordinary population.

It would certainly be extremely difficult to deny that there is not
some evidence that some psychopaths are suffering from actual
brain disease.

Lawyers currently turn to textbooks of psychiatry in preparing a
defense for a client in order to help them decide on the sort of
questions they want to ask the psychiatric witness and the information they expect to obtain from him. Any of our current psychiatric texts contain a section on the psychopath under one heading
or another. The new classification of the American Psychiatric Association describes sociopathic personality disturbance as follows:

Individuals placed in this category are *ill* primarily in terms of
society and of conforming with the prevailing cultural milieu and
not only in terms of personal discomfort or in relations with other
individuals. However, sociopathic reactions are very often symptomatic or severe, underlying personality disorder, neurosis, or psychosis, as a result of organic brain injury or disease.

Perhaps the most common text used on this continent is Noyes'
Modern Clinical Psychiatry (5), which says:

In a neurosis and psychosis, psychopathologically dynamic forces
find expression in the psychologic field. In psychosomatic or
psychophysiological disorder they find physiological expression in
the somatic symptom. In a sociopathic personality these forces are
expressed not in the psychologic or somatic but in the social field,
like the symptoms of the neurotic or psychosomatic patient, the behavior of the psychopath presumably has its psychogenesis and its
psychopathology.

This is followed by a whole page on the psychopathology of the
psychopath, pointing up that the dynamics are very much the same
as psychosis and neurosis and are only expressed differently. In other
words, it seems to me perfectly clear that Noyes holds the opinion
that the so-called "psychopath" (in more modern terminology,
"sociopathic personality type") is a sick person and that his sickness

is exactly the same sickness as that of the psychotic and the neurotic —the only difference being the way that the symptoms are expressed.

It is not only in Canada that this kind of difficulty exists, as is evidenced by the Blocker case heard in the United States Court of Appeals for the District of Columbia in 1957 (9). Blocker was tried and found guilty of the offense of which he was accused, but the conviction was reversed by the appeal court. Judge Berger, the circuit judge, makes this statement:

After his trial, and while his appeal was pending in this court, another case (in re Rosenfield, 157F., supp. 18) (D.D.C., 1957) was being heard on petition for release on a writ of habeas corpus. In that case a psychiatrist made it known to the District Court that between the Court session on Friday and Monday morning, St. Elizabeth's Hospital by some process then not disclosed, altered its "official" view that sociopathic or psychopathic personality disorder was *not* a mental disease. It had been decided that commencing Monday, St. Elizabeth's Hospital and its staff would thereafter call and classify the condition known to them as "psychopathic personality" as "a mental disease" or "a mental disorder."

Judge Berger adds in a footnote: "This is reminiscent of Lewis Carroll's classic utterance: 'When I use a word,' Humpty-Dumpty said, in a rather scornful tone, 'it means just what I choose it to mean—neither more nor less.' " One can sympathize with the judge's feelings, but I think that this switch of opinion by the staff of St. Elizabeth's Hospital is indicative of the difficulty that lies ahead in this field.

The next line of defense then, if we do not wish to have the psychopath considered as not responsible, lies in the definition of the word "appreciate." Can the psychopath be said to appreciate the nature and quality of his act? I am indebted to Dr. J. D. M. Griffin for the report of a case where this was argued. This article (3) reports: "The psychopathic murderer is popularly referred to as a monster or fiend. We cling to the belief in his extraordinary but self-controllable wickedness for that is the only way that we can explain him and still condemn him to death for the show of legality and an easy conscience." The article goes on to point out that under the present law in Great Britain any other interpretation cannot be arrived at but that the United States is moving more satisfactorily in a more humane and just direction—apparently where the psychopathic murderer will be considered as sick and not as a criminal. It would appear that following the British Act in 1957 the United States is pretty much where it was in 1955 while definite changes have occurred in the United Kingdom.

The *New Statesman* article reports on one Dolfi Salinger who was found not guilty in the Maryland courts, by reason of insanity, to a number of charges of armed robbery. He was first seen by a Mr. Abraham, a social worker with the Jewish Big Brothers League of Baltimore, who started the ball rolling by remarking simply and naively—"personally, I think you're crazy." Abraham was able to get together a group of Baltimore citizens who "for public spirited and scientific reasons were interested in helping with Dolfi's defense." Dr. Robert N. Linder and Dr. E. Wilkinson of the Spring Grove State Hospital both agreed that Dolfi had "all the classic symptoms of the aggressive, antisocial psychopath." They were supported by a third psychiatrist, Dr. Edward F. Curren, who examined Dolfi at the jail and held the view that: "A psychopath of Dolfi's type wears only the mask of sanity, that though he may not be psychotic in the ordinary sense of suffering from visual or auditory hallucinations, his condition is equivalent to a psychosis."

One of Baltmore's most experienced trial lawyers was briefed for Dolfi's defense and the psychiatric witnesses were interested enough to make no charge for their services. Dr. Manfred Guttmacher appeared for the prosecution. The statement is made:

It is obvious reading through Dr. Guttmacher's testimony that he was probably speaking in sympathy and agreement with the defendant psychiatrist. The only essential point of dispute concerned the meaning of the word "know" under the M'Naghten Rules. Dr. Guttmacher defined it in a purely cognitive sense. The defense psychiatrist argued that knowing is not exclusively a function of the intellect but must be considered in terms of a total personality. The defense had support from members of Dolfi's family who all testified that he was insane and incapable of distinguishing right from wrong, and it could not be shaken under cross examination.

The jury took just over two hours to reach their verdict, which was not guilty by reason of insanity.

It is my guess that they would have reached their verdict in two minutes if the defense attorney had been able to use the word "appreciate" as he can in Canada and the judge had instructed the jury in the full sense of this. This article concludes with an enthusiastic account of what will result from Dolfi's treatment which some of us might accept with a grain of salt. Nevertheless, it points to what is going to happen regarding this question of whether the psychopath has a mental illness or not and whether he appreciates the nature and quality of his act.

Elaborating the question of appreciation, can it be honestly said that the psychopath does appreciate the nature and quality of his act as we are told the jurisprudence defines it. Certainly, it seems to me that it is just in this realm of appreciation that the defect of the psychopath lies. There is no supportive literature which can make it very easy to defend the proposition that the psychopath has normal appreciation.

Turning to Noyes (5) again, I find this statement:

Typically, he is characterized by an emotional immaturity reflected by his impulsive and instant response to his feelings. The psychopath lacks a conscience due possibly to an emotional deprivation in childhood which made it impossible to identify himself with any parental figure. Emotional and personality development lags. Many psychopaths, while not intellectually deficient, seem emotionally such. They, therefore, lack keenness and delicacy of sentiment.

A few sentences down the page, Noyes says: "He has no critical awareness of his motives and lacks foresight in discriminating reflective judgment. He is unable to judge his own behavior from another's standpoint." Surely this is the very essence of the definition "appreciate" which is laid down in our jurisprudence. Later it is stated:

The psychopath lacks purpose, aim, and foresight, is deficient in a sense of responsibility, and lives for the moment. He demands immediate and instant gratification of his desires with no concern as to the feelings and interest of others with whom he forms few emotional relationships or stable affectionate ties. He does not build up a sense of social values as normally should occur through the process of identification. As a result, such a sense is frequently distorted. The demands of instinct are not adjusted to the demands of society.

It would seem to me then that more and more we are moving to the point where the psychopath will have a defense and will probably no longer be looked on by the law as responsible for his acts.

No change was introduced into Canadian law as a result of the report of the McRuer Commission. There has, however, been an important change in Canadian criminal law resulting from the passing of Bill C-92 to amend the Criminal Code as to capital and noncapital murder. This appears in our Criminal Code as Section 202A. I should say that I have discussed the import of this amendment with a number of lawyers and find that they have considerable doubts as to its exact meaning. Canadians will remember that at the time this amendment was debated by the Senate, a number of the leading experts in criminal law from Canadian universities argued very strongly that this amendment was unclear, lent itself to misinterpretation, and would tend to confuse the administration of justice rather than be helpful. However, to a psychiatrist with little sophistication in the nicety of law it does seem that the introduction of noncapital murder will sharply reduce the appearance of psychiatrists in court. Generally, in murder trials the psychiatrist is only called when the accused is in danger of being found guilty and receiving a capital sentence. If it did not sound too facetious, one might say that no murderer in his right mind would plead insanity unless there was danger of hanging. In most of Canada, the verdict of not guilty because of insanity carries with it the certainty of confinement to a provincial mental hospital for life. Now with the introduction of noncapital murder, a great many charges will lie in this area and will not carry the death sentence. The prisoner who is found guilty of noncapital murder will receive a prison sentence in circumstances which are frequently much more comfortable and pleasant than a provincial mental hospital and, with good behavior, for a much shorter time.

Capital murder, as I understand it, is now reduced to three situations:

1. Planned and deliberate murder,
2. When the murder occurs in the course of other crimes; for example, armed robbery, rape, etc.
3. When the murder results in the death of a police officer, warden, jailer, etc., who is exercising his duties.

It would seem then that most of the murders in which the psychiatrist is asked to testify fall into the noncapital group and that the shadow of the scaffold will no longer be ominously present in such proceedings. Hopefully, then, the psychiatrist may be called not as a last trench defense, but rather when the judge or crown has an honest doubt regarding the mental state of the accused.

The one place where this pious hope is likely to break down is again in connection with the psychopath who is likely to become involved in armed robbery, rape, etc., and under such circumstances, may pull the trigger of the gun. I have already outlined in some detail my feelings regarding the kind of defense that this person will have; and, as I have indicated, I expect to see it raised as an issue in Canadian courts more and more frequently in the next few years.

Before concluding this report on the relationship of psychiatry and the law in Canada, there are several other points I would like to mention. The first is the frequent commutation of the death sentence in Canada through the right of the royal prerogative of mercy or commutation by the Governor in Council. The mechanisms by which this is achieved are not generally known to psychiatrists. They provide an excellent safeguard against the miscarriage of justice and, indeed, generally lead, in the language of the Interpretation Act, to a fair, large, and liberal enforcement of the codified laws. Within two weeks following a verdict of guilty in a capital case, the trial judge is required to send to the minister of justice a report containing a substantial summary of the salient facts of the case together with any remarks or recommendations he may wish to make with reference to the exercise of executive clemency. The minister of justice then will receive a complete transcript of the evidence, the trial judge's charge to the jury, and the trial judge's personal, detailed observations regarding medical testimony, the issue of insanity, or his own observations of the prisoner. This is supplemented by any reports which may come from the jail, the prison physician, etc. This is then reviewed in the Department of Justice and a report made to the Governor General in Council. If there is any question as to the prisoner's mental condition, the minister may, and very frequently does, appoint a psychiatrist to examine the evidence and the prisoner.

At the time of the Royal Commission, the Honorable Mr. Garson, minister of justice at that time, gave a detailed statement showing the very careful inquiry carried out by his department in regard to these examinations. Mr. Garson stated: "The point that I wish to make here is that no detail is ever considered too trivial where the life of the condemned person is concerned to merit the most comprehensive inquiry and investigation" (2). Mr. Garson also noted that this procedure allowed the minister and his department to consider a great many facts which could not be admitted to a court of law because of the rules of evidence. This frequently resulted in commutation of sentence, and I think it impressively convinced the commission that it is exceedingly difficult to be hanged in Canada under any circumstances and that this provision for commutation of sentence gave an added safeguard to the patient with psychiatric difficulty. This was well expressed by the minister when he said (2):

> But if there appears to have been nevertheless a degree of abnormality sufficient to affect materially the control of his conduct, especially when he was under great mental stress or emotional strain, the tendency depending, of course, upon the facts of the case under review would be to exercise clemency by way of commutation.

That this was not the view of Mr. Garson and the government that he represented is shown by the record of the succeeding government when commutation of sentence was so frequent that it frequently involved political criticism. From the time the Progressive Conservative government succeeded the Liberal government, represented by Mr. Garson, until July 13, 1961, 42 out of 54 death sentences were commuted. Nevertheless, it would be my belief that in this regard the government was interpreting the will of most of the Canadian people who have shown themselves to look with disfavor on capital punishment. I believe that this legal provision has worked well and justly in recent years. I have no reason to believe that it has not previously worked equally well and been equally just. However, there is some feeling that full utilization of this procedure depends to a very considerable extent on the attitude of the minister of justice and members of his department. The Royal Commission felt that this review should be obligatory rather than depend upon the attitudes of any group of people. Their recommendation is of interest.

Our conclusion is that the practice outlined by Mr. Garson for securing psychiatric assistance in capital cases should be provided for by statute and not left to the decision of the responsible Minister. Where insanity has been an issue at the trial or where the Minister has any reason to believe that the person under sentence of death is or may have been suffering from a disease of the mind, statutory provision should be made that the Minister shall appoint a board of three psychiatrists to examine the condemned person and report. We did not think the examination should be confined to the mental condition at the time the examination takes place. In addition to considering degrees of mental disease which may not come within the laws defined, evidence might well be available to such a body that could not come before a court under the rules of evidence which must apply in all criminal cases. For example, family history and copies of hospital records are often important; but such evidence in many cases might not be obtainable through channels provided by law. Because of poverty or many other reasons, including the difficulty of getting evidence at home or from abroad in such a form as to be admissable at the trial, we think such a review would be a humane measure to safeguard against any error that might take place at the trial.

This is surely a very sensible recommendation and one which would complete the many safeguards that have been erected to deal with such problems in Canada.

Finally, what of the prisoner who has been found not guilty because of insanity. It was rather astonishing that a number of well-informed people appeared before the commission with the idea that such a verdict freed the person and allowed him to return to the community. This mistaken belief seems to be one of the main reasons that many members of the public are against modification of the laws of criminal responsibility. Nothing, of course, could be further from the truth. The verdict of not guilty because of insanity carries with it a certain commitment to a provincial mental hospital to await the lieutenant governor's pleasure before his release. In point of fact, this means that he is sent to a mental hospital; and in many cases even though he has medically made a good recovery, he will have great difficulty gaining his release. One suspects that whether or not he gains his release will depend to a very considerable extent upon the amount of pressure which is brought to bear by relatives and other interested parties, and the amount of community uproar that has resulted from the nature of the crime committed. The problem of the release of such patients is a provincial responsibility rather than a federal. The commission suggested that it would be wise if the provincial authorities set up some regular review of all cases committed to a mental hospital on a lieutenant governor's warrant. If following such a review, it was determined that the patient had recovered from his mental disease, then provision should be made for his release. At the time of these hearings, the province of Saskatchewan was the only province having such legislation; and in this province it seemed to work very well. In other provinces, there was a good deal of evidence that many patients languished in mental hospitals far longer than was necessary, that this was frequently due to a feeling that their release was entirely dependent upon physicians employed by the government, and that any mistakes that were made would reflect on the government. It was suggested that the board which should be set up to inquire into such matters should include nongovernment psychiatrists whose action could not be criticized in terms of government policy.

One further observation regarding the relationship between psychiatry and law in Canada: despite all that has been written previously, there are a fair number of prisoners who at the present moment cannot be said to be completely irresponsible and who, even if the suggestion regarding diminished responsibility were put into effect, would still receive a lesser sentence but would spend some time in one of the penitentiaries of Canada. Such persons who have frequently diagnosable mental disorders certainly have the right to psychiatric surveillance and, if possible, treatment during their period in the penitentiary. Indeed, with the psychiatrically disturbed prisoner, his mental condition is likely to become much worse if such is not provided. This has been noted in Canada for a good many years—in fact, ever since the Archambault Report (6) in 1938. This report recommended psychiatrists and the opportunity for psychiatric treatment in all of the penitentiaries of Canada. Like so many reports of Canadian commissions, this, too, has not proved very effective; and there are very few psychiatrists working in the penitentiaries of Canada. Most penitentiaries have no psychiatric help at all; and where such is available, the psychiatrist has such a huge task that there is little aid that he can give. There is the need to strengthen radically the psychiatric staffs of penitentiaries. In this regard some may feel that many of the psychiatric problems in the penitentiary are not capable of being dealt with by any currently available techniques. This, I believe, is true; and it does point up the need for very careful and exhaustive research in this field. This is an area which has hardly been explored at all and one which demands the attention of all interested parties.

SUMMARY

This paper attempts to give a picture of the relationships between psychiatry and law which exist in the Dominion of Canada. The information has largely been taken from the report of the Royal Commission on Insanity as a Defense in Criminal Law under the Honorable Chief Justice McRuer. Many of the interpretations are the author's and he and not the commission must assume responsibility for the opinions stated previously. It is my impression that in Canada we have a situation which provides a satisfactory working relationship between the lawyer and the psychiatrist. This is not perfect, and suggestions are made for its improvement. The most vital step would be a better appreciation by both professions of the attitudes and viewpoints of the other. There is also a great deal of knowledge that could be shared between the two professions. An extension of psychiatric teaching in the law schools and legal teaching in our residency programs for psychiatrists would do a good deal toward improving the situation and assuring that some of the remaining difficulties could be constructively dealt with in the future.

REFERENCES

1. Curran, D., and Partridge, M. *Psychological Medicine* (4th ed.). Edinburgh: E. & S. Livingstone, Ltd., 1955, p. 106.
2. Garson, S. C. Royal Commission on the Law of Insanity as a Defense in Criminal Cases, p. 3.
3. Griffin, J. D. M. Anticipating Murder. *The New Statesman and The Nation,* December 3, 1955.
4. Guttmacher, M., and Weihofen, H. *Psychiatry and the Law.* New York: W. W. Norton & Co., 1952.
5. Noyes, A. P., and Kolb, L. C. *Modern Clinical Psychiatry* (5th ed.). Philadelphia: W. B. Saunders Co., 1958, p. 546.
6. *Report of the Royal Commission to Investigate the Penal System of Canada.* London: King's Printer, 1938.
7. Royal Commission on the Law of Insanity as a Defense in Criminal Cases (Canada) 1954-1956. Ottawa: Queen's Printer, 1956.
8. Stephen, J. *History of the Criminal Law of England* (vol. 2) London: Macmillan & Company, 1883, p. 174.
9. United States Court of Appeals for the District of Columbia Circuit, No. 15777. *Comer Blocker,* Appellant v. *United States of America,* Appellee, 1957.
10. Walker, N. M'Naghten's Ghost. *The Listener,* August 29, 1963.
11. Zilboorg, G. *The Psychology of the Criminal Act and Punishment.* New York: Harcourt, Brace & World, 1954.

Tests To Determine Responsibility for Criminal Acts

CLARENCE B. FARRAR

The first useful criterion for assessing responsibility for a criminal act, was formulated by a panel of British judges in 1843 in response to five questions put to them by the House of Lords after considerable debate revealing conflicting opinions. Jurisprudence, in the words of Maudsley (3) writing in 1874, had been, previous to 1843, "in a very defective state."

In view of the consequence of these questions and the judges' answers it seems desirable to give the substance of both.

First: What is the law respecting alleged crimes committed by persons afflicted with insane delusion, in respect of one or more particular subjects or persons; for example, where the accused knew he was acting contrary to law, but did the act, under the influence of insane delusion, to redress supposed grievance or injury, or of producing some public benefit?

Answer: Assuming that the inquiries are confined to persons laboring under such partial delusions only, and not in other respects insane, we are of the opinion that under the conditions mentioned he is nevertheless punishable, according to the crime, if he knew that he was acting contrary to the law of the land.

Second: What are the proper questions to be put to the jury when a person alleged to be afflicted with insane delusion of the character mentioned is charged with a crime (for example, murder) and insanity is set up as a defense?

Third: In what terms ought the question to be left to the jury as to the prisoner's state of mind at the time of the crime?

Answer to second and third questions: That the jury ought to be told that every man is presumed to be sane and to possess sufficient reason to be responsible for his crimes, until the contrary be proved to their satisfaction; and that to establish a defense on the ground of insanity it must be clearly proved that, at the time of the crime the accused was laboring under such a defect of reason, from disease of the mind, as not to know the nature and quality of the act he was doing, or, if he did know it, that he did not know he was doing what was wrong; wrong, that is, in respect to the very act with which he is charged. If the accused was conscious that the act was one which he ought not to do, and if that act was also contrary to the law of the land, he is punishable.

Fourth: If a person under an insane delusion as to the existing facts commits an offense in consequence thereof, is he thereby excused?

Answer: The answer must depend on the nature of the delusion. If he labors under such partial delusion as we assumed before, and is not in other respects insane, he must be considered in the same situation as to responsibility, as if the facts, with respect to which the delusion exists, were real. If under the influence of delusion the accused believed his life to be threatened and killed his supposed attacker in self-defense, he would not be punishable. If, however, the delusion was that only his character and fortune had been seriously injured, and he has killed in revenge for the supposed injury, he would be punishable.

Fifth: Can a medical man, conversant with the disease of insanity, who never saw the prisoner previous to the trial, but who was present during the whole trial and the examination of all witnesses, be asked his opinion as to the state of the prisoner's mind at the time of the alleged crime, or his opinion whether he was then conscious that he was acting contrary to law, or whether he was then laboring under any and what delusion?

Answer: We think the medical man in the circumstances mentioned cannot in strictness be asked his opinion in the stated terms, because each of those questions involves the determination of the truth of the facts deposed to, which is for the jury to decide, and the questions are not mere questions of science wherein such evidence is admissible.

Lord Hale had used the distinction between "a partial insanity and a total insanity . . . and this partial insanity seems not to excuse them (the offenders) in the committing of any offense for its matter capital; for, doubtless most persons that are felons of themselves and others are under a degree of partial insanity when they commit these offenses."

On the principle laid down by Lord Hale and followed in English courts, Maudsley comments: "It was thought no inhumanity towards the defects of human nature to punish as a fully responsible agent a person who was suffering from partial insanity, whatever influence the disease might have had upon his unlawful act."

Thus in a later capital case Mr. Justice Tracy observed that, to be exempted from punishment, the offender "must be a man that is totally deprived of his understanding and memory, and doth not know what he is doing, no more than an infant, than a brute or a wild beast; such a one is never the object of punishment." This ruling recognized a clear distinction between criminal and civil cases. For the former the mental test came to be referred to as the "wild beast" test.

A first step to correct the "very defective state" of jurisprudence was taken in 1800 when Erskine defended and secured the acquittal of Hadfield who was being tried for shooting at the King in Drury Lane Theater. Hadfield, who was patently insane, knew what he was doing and had purposefully planned his criminal act. It was the product of delusion and the absurdity of the "wild beast" test was made apparent; but a judicial clarification of criteria of responsibility was not yet established.

In fact, in a case in 1812 in which Bellingham was being tried for the murder of Mr. Spencer Percival, the Home Secretary, the "right and wrong" test was made crucial. The accused, like Hadfield, was under the pressure of insane delusions, but the judicial climate had altered. Court proceedings were brief, Bellingham was convicted and executed seven days after his crime, it being held that he was able to distinguish between right and wrong in a general sense, not merely with regard to the criminal act for which he was being tried.

These two cases, Hadfield and Bellingham, illustrate the inconsistencies of judicial procedure between 1800 and 1812 in dealing with the crime of murder or attempted murder. In the eye of the law, similar cases resulted in one instance in acquittal, in the other in prompt execution.

Maudsley sums up the situation: "There was no settled principle, no actual uniformity of practice, no certainty of result." Hitherto two theories, each inconsistent with the other, had been considered as tests exempting from punishment offenders charged with capital crimes—the delusional basis of motivation and the basic inability to distinguish right from wrong. The "wild beast" test was no longer appealed to, as being too gross an affront to both a moral sense and common sense.

In 1843 a further step in advance was taken. M'Naghten, under the influence of persecutory delusions, and mistaking the identity of his victim, shot and killed Mr. Edward Drummond, the private secretary of Sir Robert Peel, the man he intended to kill. The facts of the case were brought out in court and the accused was acquitted on the ground of insanity despite the fact that "M'Naghten had transacted business a short time before the deed, and had shown no obvious symptoms of insanity in his ordinary discourse and conduct." In his defense of the accused, Mr. Cockburn (later Lord Chief Justice) was able to show that for many years M'Naghten had been insane and that his insane suspicions had from time to time determined his conduct, although hitherto without serious consequences.

Now, at long last, it seemed necessary to establish definite criteria by which through legal procedure an offender should or should not be punished for his crime. It was at this juncture that the House of Lords placed before the judges the five questions referred to first. Their replies contained the statement known since as the "M'Naghten Rule." This rule has served as a test of responsibility in criminal cases in English-speaking jurisdictions since 1843. It is a long advance from the wild beast test but is not a scientific criterion or a faultless one; it has shown, however, that even an imperfect rule may be made to serve the cause of justice when applied judiciously.

The conditions of the rule have become well known during its long ascendency and may be repeated very briefly as they appear in the judges' statement: "To establish a defense on the ground of insanity it must be clearly proved that at the time of the crime the accused was laboring under such a defect of reason, from disease of the mind, as not to know the nature and quality of the act he was doing, or, if he did know it, that he did not know he was doing what was wrong."

We may well recall the judicious words of Maudsley (3): "The uprightness of English judges has happily been seldom called in question, but it may well be doubted whether the result of their solemn deliberations, as embodied in their answers to the questions put to them by the House of Lords, will commend their wisdom to the approbation of foreign nations and future ages."

Nevertheless, their answers have prevailed 320 years, despite their deficiencies and despite numerous and obvious criticisms. We remind ourselves that it is the jury that is required to render the verdict, not the expert who weighs the differential meanings of words.

It is the "right and wrong" test that has caused continuous argument; it has been pointed out that this is a question of values, a highly philosophical or metaphysical issue about which there can be no ultimate agreement. Questions of right and wrong start confidently in the kindergarten and may follow us through life. Theoretically, laws are set up to establish canons. Eventually many of them die in the statute books. The careful individual may ask himself: "Should I do this—or that?" And upon his answer may depend the issues of his life. Mercier gives a useful answer to the legal interpretation of right and wrong. Criminal responsibility, Mercier said, is being "rightly liable to punishment." But in view of the impossibility of an ultimate and universal applicability of a definition of "rightly," he added that it meant in accordance with "the body of opinion as to what is right and wrong now prevalent in my own country and generation."

Reviewing the various circumstances, as will occur to anyone, in which killing is not a crime, Clarence Darrow, the great criminal lawyer, summed the whole matter up with the precise statement: "It is wrong to kill when it is wrong to kill." In a case in court, the deciding issue, regardless of tests, may simply be the cleverness of the defense.

I once asked a leading Toronto lawyer if, in taking the defense of a capital case, he wished to know before going into court whether or not the accused had committed the offense charged. His answer was firmly in the negative. A knowledge of guilt would prejudice his conduct of the case. With another criminal lawyer the situation was different. He did know the facts in the case before the trial; it was all the more credit to his defense, therefore, that the accused was acquitted. By mere coincidence I was sitting in his office awaiting a member of his staff with whom I had an appointment. A number of the defense lawyer's friends were also there to greet him on his return from court. His appearance was greeted with jubilation. "But," asked one with inoffensive effrontery, "was he guilty or not guilty?" "Guilty as hell," replied the successful criminal lawyer.

In conversation with a widely known jurist on the fallibility of tests I asked if he thought that through inadequate defense as compared with the prosecution many innocent persons were found guilty. From his knowledge and experience, the jurist replied that such cases were extremely rare. But how about the contrary situation, that of guilty persons acquitted through clever defense maneuvers? "Ah!" he stated, "that's a very different question." No elaboration was needed.

After all, the best test is the defense lawyer himself, as exemplified by Clarence Darrow in Chicago; Earl Rogers on the West Coast; and B. B. Osler in Canada, the brilliant brother of Sir William Osler.

Maudsley (3) writing in the early 1870's said: "It is notorious that the acquittal or conviction of a prisoner, when insanity is alleged, is a matter of chance. Were the issue to be decided by tossing up a shilling, instead of by the grave procedure of a trial in court, it could hardly be more uncertain." Nevertheless, the old rule of 1843 has shown considerable stability. It is still held in the English speaking world.

But it was not followed elsewhere. In mid-nineteenth-century France the Penal Code stated: "There can be no crime nor offense if the accused was in a state of madness at the time of the act." But allowing for the concept of partial insanity, the way for conflicting opinions is still open. It might be argued that the person charged with a crime might have acted on a criminal impulse independent of his insane delusions. It could be held that the criminal act was the product of a *mens rea* in a partially insane person just as in a sane person; for, as Maudsley observes, "An insane person is not exempt from the ordinary evil passions of human nature; he may do an act out of jealousy, avarice, or revenge."

Whatever consideration the concept of partial insanity or diminished responsibility might deserve in civil cases, the question becomes more serious in a capital case where the life of the accused is at stake. It may involve hair-splitting argument over the unitary functioning of the mind and confuse rather than inform the jury.

The German Penal Code, contemporary with the French Code just mentioned, contained the following: "An act is not punishable when the person at the time of doing it was in a state of unconsciousness or of disease of mind, by which a free determination of the will was excluded." Here the situation became still more complicated. It was not only necessary to show the effect of disease of the mind but the question of free will was also involved—a question that the philosophers are still working on.

Maudsley, whose book, *Responsibility in Mental Disease,* was published in 1874, was still complaining about "the superstitious reverence with which English lawyers cling to their criterion of responsibility." However, British common sense has a way of making an imperfect rule serve when a perfect one is not attainable.

One-hundred years after legal opinions in the criminal codes of both France and Germany made mental disease as such responsible for criminal acts when such mental disease could be clearly established, the state of New Hampshire took a similar position. In the case of *State* vs. *Pike* (1870), involving a murder, the jury was instructed that matters for them to decide were the crucial questions: (1) whether the defendant was suffering from a mental disease, and (2) whether the murder was the product of that disease. In a second murder case, *State* vs. *Jones* (1871), the judge charged the jury that if "the killing was the "offspring or product of mental disease, the defendant should be acquitted."

The great virtue of these New Hampshire decisions is that they seem to embody plain common sense. The persuasive value of such arguments is very strong; but they take for granted that sanity is one thing and insanity is another. The British psychiatrist, John

Conolly (1), was a man of great common sense and great wisdom. In his *An Inquiry Concerning the Indications of Insanity* (1830), he calls attention to the unfortunate circumstance that medical men "have sought for and imagined a strong and definable boundary between sanity and insanity," and this boundary, he states, has been both "imaginary and arbitrarily placed." Inasmuch as a mental disorder may exhibit various degrees of severity, and as deviations— even abnormalities—may exist without it being possible to say that they constitute mental disorder or disease, how far along the scale of aberrancies must one go before one can say that a criminal act committed at that point is the product of mental disease? Such a situation provides ground for a "battle of the experts" that has been so much criticized.

Isaac Ray has been the most thorough and searching American critic and expositor who has dealt with the various tests of responsibility by which offenders have been found guilty or innocent. His *A Treatise on the Medical Jurisprudence of Insanity* (1838) became a generally accepted authority and provoked greatly increased discussion and reporting, especially of the relationship between crime and insanity.

In the preface to the fourth edition (1860) Isaac Ray (4) said: "Every year's experience [since the first edition] has only strengthened the conviction, that much of the common law relative to insanity, whatever other support it may have, has no foundation in the facts of science."

Dr. Ray's work was mainly responsible for the rule, new in America, adopted by the New Hampshire court in 1870 and 1871 in dealing with the two cases referred to previously. The appellate court held that the manifestations of mental disease as tests of criminal intent "are all clearly matters of evidence, to be weighed by the jury upon the question whether the act was the offspring of insanity; if it was, a criminal intent did not produce it; if it was not, a criminal intent did produce it, and it was a crime."*

This ruling established the New Hampshire position essentially

---

* *State* v. *Jones,* 50 N.H. 369, 398-399 (1871).

in agreement with the contemporary penal codes of France and Germany. It took no account of the annoying question of the point along the scale of mental deviations—from an assumed normal, to abnormal, to pathologic—at which a diagnosis of insanity could be justified.

The passage in Isaac Ray's *Treatise* (4) that presumably had a determining influence in the New Hampshire decisions deserves to be quoted:

> For admitting that the person knew he was doing wrong and contrary to law, it remains to be proved that this knowledge *embraces all the elements of responsibility.** The real question at issue is, why, with this knowledge, he should commit acts incompatible with his natural character and disposition; and the only rational answer is to say, that the action of the mental powers is disturbed by the presence of disease, whatever degree of intelligence or self-control may be left, there still remains this disturbing element, the precise influence of which never can be safely estimated . . . . To inflict upon such men the ordinary consequences of crime, is virtually to punish them for being diseased, and the utmost ingenuity of logic or metaphysics can make nothing else of it.

Incidentally, Dr. Ray has something to say about the stereotyped argument that severe punishment will deter other would-be criminals:

> The absurdity of an insane person's recognizing his own insanity, forming rules for his conduct, and acting upon them, would seem too gross to be deliberately uttered by learned dignitaries of the law, had we not abundant proof to the contrary. In point of fact, it may be safely said that not an instance can be produced, of an insane person being deterred from the commission of a criminal act by the punishment of some other insane person for a similar act, or encouraged to commit it by an example of an opposite kind.

Ray discusses at considerable length the legal tests of mental competency used in various countries to determine whether an offender should be exempt from punishment. Crucial words in his discussion are: "The law relative to insanity should be simple and

* Italics added.

easily understood." He cites the New York State statute: "No act done by a person in a state of insanity can be punished as an offense." That would seem to be a simple and clear statement, but here again the difficulty is the precise definition of insanity in the given case; for it is the jury that must render the decision and the jurymen are not experts, and the experts who may be called to assist them may be able to offer only opinions, not facts.

A surprising reaction followed a judicial decision in a court in Washington, D.C., in 1954. This involved the responsibility test in the much discussed Durham case. The court ruled that "an accused is not criminally responsible if his unlawful act was the product of mental disease or mental defect." There was nothing new about this. The court itself noted that the "new" rule was merely a restatement of the New Hampshire ruling of 1870. It is also subject to the same difficulties; and statements of fine distinctions are not too lucid. Nevertheless, the Durham Rule has been hailed as the new last word, and the presiding judge in the Durham case suddenly sprang into prominence.

The crucial test of accountability is usually invoked in capital cases in which the accused, if found guilty, will be sentenced either to death or to life imprisonment. Durham had been on trial for the lesser crime of housebreaking.

Dr. Sheldon Glueck, Roscoe Pound Professor of Law at Harvard University Law School, delivered the "Isaac Ray Award Lectures on Law and Psychiatry" for 1962. In them he discussed extensively the question of tests of accountability. In 1961, Judge Bazelon of the District of Columbia, the hero of the Durham Rule, had had the honor of delivering the "Isaac Ray Lectures." Dr. Glueck spoke respectfully of the Durham Rule, but did not hesitate to indicate its weak points, which recalled the New Hampshire ruling from which it was derived.

In offering a personal opinion on one specific point, namely the argument that the Durham Rule "grossly impairs the deterrent influence of punishment," Glueck (2) gives it as his "considered opinion after many years of research and reflection, the protective effect of the deterrent thrust of the criminal law, especially in capital cases and rape, has been overestimated. I know of no reliable proof that a severely punitive code in fact protects society more than a milder one does." He points out that this view is in keeping with the evidence gathered by the Royal Commission on capital punishment in Britain in 1953.

He also calls attention to the argument that the language of the Durham test, apparently so simple and conclusive, tends to equate mental abnormality with criminal irresponsibility disregarding the intermediate steps necessary to consider before one can reach such a conclusion. With these intermediate questions for which Durham does not provide, a sharp cross-examiner may confuse the witness and possibly even disqualify his evidence. In one case the judge instructed the jury to disregard the psychiatrist's evidence.

It goes without saying that the psychiatrist's evidence must be expressed in the simplest possible language, avoiding technical or theoretical words not likely to be understood by the man in the street or understood differently even by experts. The Durham language would seem at first glance to have met these requirements, but a second glance is sufficient to show that its statements have not simplified the problem but have oversimplified it, thus prejudicing the test. Its weaknesses have been pointed out in numerous cases in court as grounds for its rejection, the crucial question being the causal relationship of the mental disease or defect present to the criminal act. The difficulty of adjusting psychiatric terminology to tight legal requirements is recognized; but that likewise is one on which the jury must base their finding.

In his "Isaac Ray Lectures" Dr. Glueck devoted considerable time to the court ruling in the Durham case and the effect of this ruling in later cases. This text he reported "has had very hard sledding. It has been rejected by numerous scholars, by at least four United States Circuit Courts of Appeal, by the United States Court of Military Appeal, by the Supreme Court of some nineteen states." Generally throughout the United States the M'Naghten Rule of 1843 is adhered to; and this is noteworthy in view of the fact that each state exercises sovereign authority in determining responsibility for criminal acts, only New Hampshire having set up its own rules.

The difficulty of the definition of insanity remains. Many terms have been coined to characterize abnormal mental states and to determine which of them are punishable for offenses. The term "psychosis" has been applied quite widely to cases of mental disorders held to be of serious type—melancholia, mania, paranoia, dementia praecox, and its boundlessly extended successor, schizophrenia, which has become a sort of current terminology wastebasket. The person with a psychosis, therefore, could be called "insane." Conditions considered milder, such as hysteria, neurasthenia, and psychasthenia are called "neuroses"; and wordy battles have been fought to draw distinctions between psychoses and neuroses and likewise between responsibility and irresponsibility. Then there are the psychopathic personalities or psychopaths, more recently called sociopaths. Where do they belong? Glueck gives it as his opinion that the legal term "insanity" as implied in the Durham test includes cases regarded as pathologic from the psychiatric point of view, "whether their aberration is a psychosis or some other psychiatrically recognized pathological state." For support he refers to the American Psychiatric Association's *Diagnostic and Statistical Manual* (1952) which includes psychopathic or sociopathic personality in the category of mental disorders. All this does not bring us much further along in our efforts to be accurate and precise.

Standard psychiatric terminology may have statistical uses, but may be as apt to becloud as to illuminate clinical concepts. Psychiatric terminology is tricky, as evidenced by the changed diagnosis not infrequently met with as a chronic or remitting patient passes from clinic to clinic over the years.

The shrewd statement, quoted previously, of that remarkable institutional psychiatrist, John Conolly, may have been news then and should be common knowledge today. Surely most psychiatrists would agree that a sharp line between sane and insane cannot be drawn; and it seems to follow, as Glueck (2) observes, "that the search for any sharp black versus white dividing line between responsibility and irresponsibility is vain, and that we must be content with a reasonably flexible standard but one made as understandable and practical as the *mésalliance* between law and psychiatry will permit." In reconciling ourselves to this flexible standard, we may profitably keep in mind Isaac Ray's sobering words: "To persons practically acquainted with the insane mind, it is well known that in every hospital for the insane are patients capable of distinguishing between right and wrong, knowing well enough how to appreciate the nature and legal consequences of their acts, acknowledging the sanctions of religion, and never acting from irresistible impulse but deliberately and shrewdly."

Sensible of the weak points in the Durham test as well as in the M'Naghten Rule, Dr. Glueck (2) courageously attempts to introduce clarity in a version of his own. His proposed test, or instruction to the jury:

> If you are convinced that the defendant, at the time of the crime, was suffering from mental disease or defect which impairs his powers of thinking, feeling, willing or self-integration, and that such impairment probably made it impossible for him to understand or control the act he is charged with as the ordinary, normal person understands and controls his acts, you should find him *Not guilty on the ground of insanity*.
>
> If you are convinced that the defendant, at the time of the crime, was suffering from mental disease or defect which impaired his powers of thinking, feeling, willing or self-integration, *but you doubt* whether such impairment probably made it impossible for him to understand or control the act he is charged with as the ordinary, normal person understands and controls his acts, you should find him only *Partially responsible*.
>
> If you are convinced that the defendant was not suffering from mental disease or defect at the time of the crime, you should find him *Guilty*.

But Glueck does not seem completely satisfied with his test as stated previously, and would like to take note, if acceptable to the court, "of certain fundamentals of latter-day psychiatry." He suggests, for the guidance of the jury, the following at the end of the test:

> In considering your verdict, you are instructed that the law recognizes that mental disorder involves the total personality and not separate segments without influence on one another. You are further instructed that motives for conduct can be either conscious or

unconscious. Finally, you are instructed that in some mental illnesses various physiological or neurological disturbances can bring about psychological and behavioral disorders.

Taken together this could hardly be called a short test or be considered to follow exactly the axiom of Isaac Ray that "the law relative to insanity should be simple and easily understood." When a jury is addressed in over-learned language they may be excused if they come back for further instruction. However, Glueck's proposals have been carefully thought out and will no doubt receive studied consideration.

It should be noted that he favors and recommends the concept of diminished or partial responsibility as was proposed by Grasset many years ago. This view of Dr. Glueck is, of course, an expression of his humane attitude toward offenders generally. "In homicide cases," he states, "the chief consequence of the mid-verdict would be to remove mentally defective, sociopathic, prepsychotic and extreme long-standing neurotic offenders from the class subject to the indignity and disgrace of capital punishment or hopeless life imprisonment . . . . Such persons will of course remain hospitalized until certified and found to be no longer dangerous so far as mental illness is concerned." "Certified and found" is a strong expression, and a conscientious physician could probably be, in most cases, loath to use it over his signature. Not infrequently the newspapers remind us that a patient discharged from a mental hospital, after being so "certified and found," commits a murder. Partial responsibility or partial irresponsibility is a very contentious concept and has not been widely recognized in United States courts.

In Canada a unique and most valuable document is the *Report of the Royal Commission on the Law of Insanity as Defense in Criminal Cases,* published by the Queen's Printer in 1954. The inquiry and findings of the Royal Commission, of which the Honorable J. C. McRuer, Chief Justice of the High Court for Ontario, was Chairman, are authoritatively dealt with in another chapter in this volume by Dr. Robert O. Jones, Professor of Psychiatry, Dalhousie University, and a member of the Royal Commission. The present section should be read, therefore, in connection with Dr. Jones' presentation. Here, for the sake of completeness, only the conclusions of the Royal Commission as affecting possible changes in the Criminal Code of Canada will be set down. Their conclusions represent the interpretation of the Royal Commission of the views and usages in both law and psychiatry throughout the Dominion. This chapter, XVII of the Royal Commission report, should be read in its entirety.

It should be understood that the Canadian Criminal Code applies with equal force in all ten provinces, in contradistinction to the situation in the United States where each state makes its own criminal laws.

The points crucial for our purpose in the report of the Royal Commission are:

1. *Irresistible impulse.* "The addition of a defense of irresistible impulse related to disease of the mind would not be a wise amendment to the Criminal Code."

2. *The New Hampshire Law or the Durham Rule.* "The repeal of Section 16 and the substitution of the law of the State of New Hampshire or that of the District of Columbia would not make for a better administration of justice in Canada." (Two of the five commissioners dissented.)

3. *Diminished responsibility.* "The law of diminished responsibility should not be adopted in Canada." (Two commissioners dissented.)

4. *A board to review persons sentenced to death.* Statutory provision should be made for a board of review consisting of three psychiatrists to report to and advise the executive on the mental condition of all persons condemned to death."

Thus, insofar as the government of Canada is concerned, the Royal Commission did not recommend the adoption of either of the controversial issues of an irresistible impulse or of diminished responsibility as legally valid in a defense on the ground of insanity. Likewise, the Royal Commission found against the adoption of the New Hampshire Law of 1870–1871 or the ruling in the Durham case in the District of Columbia in 1954 in a defense on the ground of insanity.

It is worth mentioning, as the Royal Commission did mention in an appendix to its report, that in the United States where degrees of murder are recognized (although there is only one degree of death in the case of the victim), the states of Connecticut, Illinois, Rhode Island, Utah, Virginia, and Wisconsin "have recognized the principle of diminished responsibility in cases of mental weakness falling short of legal insanity and reduced the conviction in such a case to second degree murder." It is also noteworthy that at the annual meeting of the Canadian Bar Association in 1963 it was urged that an amendment to the criminal code be adopted recognizing diminished responsibility in cases of mental deviation short of insanity.

One chapter in the appendix to the report of the Royal Commission is titled "Diminished Responsibility"; and, in addition to the states where this principle is recognized, the chapter deals also with the application of diminished responsibility elsewhere, particularly in England and Scotland. In Scotland the law comes to the point without waste of words. As used there, it is "a device to enable the courts to take account of a special category of mitigating circumstances in cases of murder and to avoid passing sentence of death in cases where such circumstances exist."

In a second appendix to the report of the McRuer Commission is a summary of conclusions and recommendations of the Royal Commission on capital punishment in Great Britain (1949–1953). We quote two items:

We consider (with one dissentient) that the text of responsibility laid down in England by the M'Naghten Rules is so defective that the law on the subject ought to be changed.

If an alteration were to be made by extending the scope of the rules, we suggest that a formula on the following lines should be adopted:

The jury must be satisfied that, at the time of committing the act, the accused, as a result of disease of the mind or mental deficiency, (a) did not know the nature and quality of the act or (b) did not know that it was wrong or (c) was incapable of preventing himself from committing it.

Although this formula might not prove wholly satisfactory, we consider (with one dissentient) that it would be better to amend the rules in this way than to leave them as they are.

As this book reflects mainly Canadian usage and opinion we may again refer to two striking conclusions of the McRuer Commission. Under clause (c) in the British formula just cited, rather unconvinced allowance is made for the "irresistible impulse." The Canadian Royal Commission concluded (with no dissentients): "the addition of a defense of irresistible impulse related to disease of the mind would not be a wise amendment to the Criminal Code."

And further, as has been noted, the Royal Commission concluded (with two dissentients): "the law of diminished responsibility should not be adopted in Canada." Here it may be suggested that the ground is a little more open, as indicated by the fact that two of the five commissioners dissented.

It is a matter of common clinical observation that just as there are degrees of mental ability, this is only another way of saying that there are degrees of mental incapacity as, for example, in the recognized levels of mental deficiency, or "mental retardation" as it is referred to mainly in the United States. But this clinical fact may conceivably be subject to abuse if used as a defense in a capital case.

In their Memorandum of Dissent the two dissenting commissioners state:

> We believe that the evidence shows that there are degrees of mental deficiency or mental illness not sufficient to absolve persons from all responsibility for criminal offenses but sufficient nevertheless to make such persons not fully accountable for their actions. We recommend [amendment] to provide for the operation of the doctrine of diminished responsibility, as practiced in Scotland [quoted previously], in cases where there is evidence of mental deficiency or disease of the mind falling short of the full defense of insanity.

In summing up, it is not a little surprising that the grossly imperfect M'Naghten Rule of 1843 should have remained authoritative essentially unchanged throughout the English-speaking countries. Maudsley had ridiculed the M'Naghten formula; and while its defects were recognized as successive innovators have continued to propose new tests, one defeatist judgment is recalled which may be the best statement of the situation that has been made to date and ranks with those of Isaac Ray.

In the second New Hampshire case, *State* v. *Jones* (1871), Judge Ladd comments on the answers of the English judges to the questions put to them by the House of Lords, and on the doctrine that developed therefrom as an accepted legal principle which has persisted.

A remark by the great teacher, Emil Kraepelin, so clear and simple and obvious as to be easily passed over, and even forgotten, may profitably be recalled. He constantly reminded his students and readers that he who undertakes to look into the mind of another and discern its inner workings is *undertaking a very difficult problem.* And yet rules are laid down by which mental experts or laymen are asked to determine the sequence of intrapsychic events of the accused—not at the time of the examination, but at the moment the offense was committed, hours, days, or weeks earlier.

Judge Ladd's conclusion deserves emphasis: "It is a question of fact whether any universal test exists, and it is also a question of fact what that test is, if any there be." Presumably Judge Ladd would not have been one to attempt to formulate such a test.

But to return to the 121-year-old rule that has come to be almost proverbial despite the most destructive criticism, we may note that the McRuer Commission did not dislodge it, but merely substituted the word "appreciate" for the word "know" in the phrase, "did not know the nature and quality of the act." It was held that the word "appreciate" indicated a more precise and fuller knowledge than the word "know." For authority, the *New Oxford Dictionary* revealed that the former term has five different uses depending upon the context. The one applicable to the present statute is: "To estimate aright, to perceive the full force of." In the revised Criminal Code of Canada which came into effect April 1, 1955, the word "appreciate" replaces "know" in the rule. It is recalled that not all American jurists take account of this rather fine distinction.

At any rate the words used in the original rule deserve notice. The question of accountability for a criminal act hangs between two conditions: knowledge of the *nature and quality* of the act, or knowledge that it was *wrong*. Of the 31 words containing the core of the test, all but 3 are words of one syllable. The test is expressed in basic English and would appear to be easily understood. The contradiction, possibly overlooked, between the two conditions would presumably not be taken into serious account by the jury. They seem to have escaped the notice even of the learned judges who, with due deliberation, framed their answers that constituted the test. Granting that the purpose was to construct a statement that was simple, short, and easily grasped, it seems clear that the phraseology adopted should represent ordinary common sense; it was plain talk such as would appeal to the general public from which the jury was drawn.

Take the question of right and wrong. It would be understood that this did not involve an incursion into the abstraction of ethics or philosophy. It concerned only the right or wrong of the particular act. And even so, making allowance for the relativity of the concept, for example, of the right to kill a person who is threatening your life, we can fall back on Mercier's pragmatic definition, already alluded to, which is also plain common sense. It seems a fair question whether the short words and the simple and understandable language of the Rule of 1843, in spite of its defects, may not largely account for its durability and its usefulness.

This paper is not a brief for the M'Naghten Rule, but simply a recognition that it works, and has done so for a long time; and a recognition in presumptive agreement with Judge Ladd that, considering what it is that has to be judged and upon which accountability depends, a perfect test is not likely to be found.

ADDENDUM

Through the kindness of Mrs. Phyllis Woodward, Legal Assistant to the Medical Director, American Psychiatric Association, Washington, D.C., recent information has been received concerning the assessment of responsibility of the individual for criminal acts.

The Durham Rule, which became effective in the District of Columbia in 1954, is still the law in that District. Efforts in Congress to have the Durham Rule rescinded in the District of Columbia have thus far failed.

Maine is the only state in which the Durham Rule is in force. It was adopted by Statute in that state in 1961. No other jurisdiction has adopted the Durham Rule by statute or decision.

Diminished Responsibility. While in most jurisdictions the status of diminished responsibility is not authorized by Statute, Weihofen (5) reports that the following states recognize Diminished Responsibility in criminal cases in which the mental status is in question: California, Colorado, Connecticut, Tennessee, Indiana, Ohio, Rhode Island, Utah, Wisconsin; and perhaps also Kentucky, Oregon, and Montana.

REFERENCES

1. Conolly, J. *An Inquiry Concerning the Indications of Insanity.* London: Dawsons of Pall Mall, 1964. (First published in 1830, now reprinted by photolithography.)
2. Glueck, S. *Law and Psychiatry.* Baltimore: The Johns Hopkins Press, 1962.
3. Maudsley, H. *Responsibility in Mental Disease.* London: Henry L. King & Co., 1874.
4. Ray, I. *A Treatise on the Medical Jurisprudence of Insanity* (4th ed.). Boston: Little, Brown and Co., 1860.
5. Weihofen, H. *The Urge to Punish.* New York: Farrar, Straus & Cudahy, 1957, chapter 5, footnote 26.

CHILD PSYCHIATRY

The Cytogenetics of Mongolism

JAMES R. MILLER AND FRED J. DILL

INTRODUCTION

Although mongolism is probably an extremely old disease, apparently having occurred in the Saxons (5), a first attempt at a clinical description was made by Down as late as 1866 (11). From that date until 1959, the etiology of the condition was a challenge to many students of human biology. Recently, Warkany (39) compiled a list of 39 etiological theories proposed during this period. All except one of these were insufficient in explaining the many peculiar aspects of mongolism, some of which are discussed here.

Maternal Age

Shortly after Down's description, it was observed that mongols tend to be the last born in their sibships. This was confirmed many times but it was never clear whether the association was with birth order or with maternal or paternal age since all three variables are highly correlated. The development of proper statistical procedures by Jenkins (18) and Penrose (22) indicated that the correlation was with maternal age.

Incidence

Mongolism occurs approximately once in 600 births in Caucasian populations (9, for review). As indicated previously, this incidence

This paper is dedicated to Professor Bruce D. Graham in sincere appreciation of his stimulation and guidance during his tenure as Head of the Department of Paediatrics in the University of British Columbia.

The original work reported in this review was supported by a grant from the Vancouver Foundation and a National Health Grant (Canada).

127

rate is not constant over all maternal ages. As is shown in Figure 1, the rate for the age groups under 20 years is approximately 0.5 per 1000. There is a gradual increase in this rate until age 30, when there is a sharp rise to approximately 2 per 1000 at age 35–39 and 8 per 1000 or over in the over-40 age group. These rates, derived from

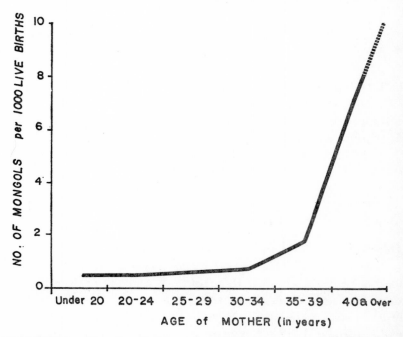

FIGURE 1. *Graph showing incidence rates of mongolism at different maternal ages, based on statistics obtained in the Province of British Columbia 1955–1960, inclusive.*

statistics gathered in the Province of British Columbia (29), are in good agreement with those of Penrose (24) for an English population and of Collmann and Stoller (10) for Victoria, Australia.

Penrose (24) has suggested that the maternal age distribution curve is bimodal and, in fact, comprises two populations: a large age-dependent and a small age-independent group.

Familial Occurrence

The recurrence of mongolism in a sibship is a rare event. In such sibships, the mean maternal age is slightly but significantly lower than the mean maternal age in mongolism generally. In addition, this same effect is observed when an affected individual occurs in a collateral relative on the maternal side of the pedigree but not when such an individual occurs on the paternal side (23). On the basis of reports in the literature on the offspring of female mongols, it would appear that the risk of mongolism in such offspring is about 50 percent, since 5 out of 12 infants have been affected.

Microstigmata

Related to the observations on familial occurrence are those associated with the presence in normal close relatives of some affected individuals of characteristic minor signs of mongolism such as epicanthic folds, fissured tongue, transverse palmar flexion creases, and dermatoglyphic patterning. When they do occur, such microstigmata appear to be more frequent in siblings and maternal relatives (24, 39, for reviews).

Twins

Allen and Baroff (1) have reviewed the literature relating to the occurrence of mongolism in twins. There appears to be about 4 percent concordance for the defect among dizygotic pairs and probably 100 percent concordance among monozygotic pairs. The significance of this observation is that monogolism must be determined in monozygotic twins before the earliest time at which the zygote may divide into two individuals; certainly within the first week of gestation.

Among the many theories of the etiology of mongolism advanced prior to 1959, the one which might reasonably explain all of these aspects of the disease was that relating to chromosomal aberrations. The possibility that such genetic mechanims might be the causal factor in mongolism was first suggested by Waardenburg (38) in 1932. In his book, *Das menschliche Auge und seine Erbanlangen,* he wrote:

I should like to suggest that cytologists investigate whether, in this specific case, it is not possible that there occurs in man an example of a chromosomal aberration. Why should this not also apply to human beings; and why should it not be possible that, when this chromosomal aberration has no lethal effect, it should cause a remarkable anomaly of the constitution? Investigations should be undertaken to find out whether in mongols we are perhaps dealing with a "chromosomal deficiency" by "nondisjunction" or on the contrary with a "chromosomal duplication" (translation, 20).

Waardenburg then went on to say that the testing of this theory should not be too difficult. As it turned out, it was not possible to test the theory for 25 years. To understand this long time lag, it is necessary to know something of the history of human cytogenetics.

HUMAN CYTOGENETICS

This section is based largely on the excellent review of the subject by Stern (33) and those readers who are interested should refer to this paper for further details.

Human chromosomes were first clearly observed in 1879. However, it was not until the early 1920's that some agreement was reached on the number of chromosomes possessed by man. This number was 48. Then, for a period of 25–30 years, the field of human cytogenetics lay dormant. Anyone interested in the fundamental aspects of chromosome structure and mechanics would certainly not have chosen vertebrate material with which to work. The large complements and the "stickiness" of mammalian chromosomes discouraged cytogeneticists and, therefore, although it was generally recognized that chromosomal aberrations almost certainly occurred in man, the basic studies of chromosomal behavior were carried out in plants and insects in which the returns were more rewarding.

After a long period of quiescence, interest in the chromosomes of human beings was stimulated by two advances in cytological investigation. The first of these was the development of newer techniques in tissue culture and the study of cells grown under in vitro conditions. The second was the finding, by Dr. Murray Barr and his associates at the University of Western Ontario, of a morphologic difference between the cells of human males and females (2)—the chromatin mass and its postulated relation to the X chromosome.

This period of renewed interest in human chromosomes culminated in 1956 with a publication by Tjio and Levan (36). These botanical cytologists prepared cultures of lung fibroblasts from four therapeutically aborted embryos and observed that the vast number of cells contained 46 chromosomes, not the universally accepted 48.

To those who are not familiar with the aforementioned history, it may seem peculiar that such a fundamental biological parameter as the number of chromosomes possessed by human beings should suddenly be challenged. If a comparison is made between the chromosome preparations presented by Tjio and Levan and those available prior to their publication, some realization can be gained of the tremendous advance which this work represented and why it made such an impact on the whole of human genetics.

It should be stressed that this breakthrough did not result from the development of any new, elegant microscopy. The preparations of Tjio and Levan were viewed under an ordinary light microscope. The differences resided in the techniques of preparation, and particularly in the use of hypotonic solution and colchicine pretreatment, which resulted in a better spreading and contraction of the chromosomes.

The findings of Tjio and Levan were soon confirmed and then it was possible to test the hypothesis of Waardenburg relating to the chromosomal etiology of mongolism.

TYPES OF CHROMOSOMAL
ABERRATIONS IN MONGOLISM
Trisomy

In February 1959, Lejeune, Gautier, and Turpin (19) published their observations on the chromosomes of nine mongols (five males and four females). In all instances, there were 47 chromosomes present, the extra body being similar to one of the smallest members of the complement. Historically, it is of interest that Lejeune had completed studies on his first mongol during the summer of 1958. At the time of the Tenth International Congress of Genetics, which was held at McGill University in September of that year, he had photographs of the chromosomes of a mongol from whom tissue had been obtained for culture at autopsy. These photographs showed the presence of the small extra body. Lejeune was reluctant to present his meager findings to the Congress, but he did discuss them with a small group of staff and graduate students in the Genetics Department of McGill after the Congress had adjourned. It is interesting to speculate that if Lejeune had reported his findings at the Congress it would probably have represented the most dramatic presentation since Muller reported his observations on the effects of x-ray radiation on the genic material to the 1927 Congress.

The findings of Lejeune, Gautier, and Turpin were confirmed by Jacobs *et al.* (7), Ford *et al.* (12), and Böök *et al.* (4), all of whom

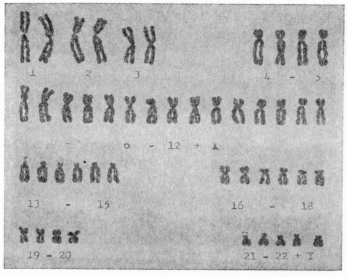

FIGURE 2. *Karyotype of a normal male. Satellites are clearly visible on four of the 13–15 chromosomes and two of the 21–22 chromosomes. The Y chromosome is the last chromosome in the karyotype; it is slightly larger than the other members of the 21–22 group and bears no satellites. The X chromosome is grouped with the 6–12 chromosomes since it cannot be accurately identified.*

suggested that the extra chromosome probably represented a trisomic state, i.e., that one of the members of the smallest group of chromosomes was present thrice, not twice, in the complement. Lejeune had termed the extra body V^h and was not clear whether this was a supernumerary chromosome unlike any member of the normal complement, or represented a trisomic state. This extra chromosome has since been observed in hundreds of mongols throughout the world and is now generally accepted as homologous to one of the normal complement. In 1960, an expert study group met in Denver to devise a system of standard nomenclature for human chromosomes (Figure 2) (30). By the terms of this nomenclature the extra chromosome observed in mongols is generally believed to be #21 (Figure 3).

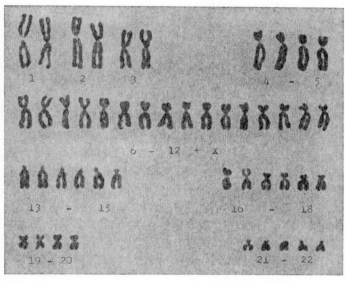

FIGURE 3. *Karyotype of a female 21 trisomic mongol. There are five chromosomes present in the 21–22 group instead of four.*

Translocations and Isochromosomes

A year after the findings outlined previously, Polani *et al.* (28) published a report entitled "A Mongol Girl with 46 Chromosomes." The patient was a typical mongol born when her mother was 21 years of age. Detailed analysis of a bone marrow culture showed only four chromosomes in the 21–22 group rather than the five which would be expected in a female mongol. In addition, there was a chromosome missing from the group now known as the 13–15 group and an extra body in the 6–12 + X group (Figure 4). The authors explained this extra body as a reciprocal translocation between a chromosome #21 and a member of the 13–15 group. Thus, the girl was considered to have effective or functional trisomy with the two

FIGURE 4. *Karyotype of a female mongol with a 13–15/21 translocation. There are only five 13–15 chromosomes and four 21–22 chromosomes, while there are seventeen in the 6–12 + X group. One of these is arbitrarily designated as the translocation chromosome and is set apart.*

visible #21 chromosomes, plus the partial #21 attached to the member of the 13–15 group. The parents of the child had normal chromosome complements.

This girl was selected for study because she had been born to a young woman. The authors reasoned that mechanisms other than trisomy might exist which could explain the occurrence of the maternal age independent class of mongolism. The presence of the translocation in this patient indicated that other mechanisms could exist. On the basis of the behavior of chromosomes with reciprocal translocations, the authors proposed the scheme presented in Figure 5. It is seen that the 13–15/21 translocation could occur in normal individuals and be transmitted. The occurrence of mongol-

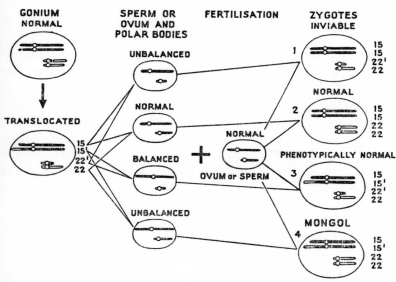

FIGURE 5. *Diagram to show the origin of the 13–15/21 translocation and its mode of inheritance. Chromosome 22 in this scheme is now classified as 21. In addition, it is now recognized that the small fusion product is lost soon after the translocation occurs. For illustration, the translocation is shown as having occurred in a spermatogonium or oogonium. In the latter case, only one of the meiotic products becomes a functional gamete; the others become polar bodies. If the translocation originated earlier in development, the change would be propagated at each mitosis and more gonia would be affected in the same way. The exact positions of breakage cannot be defined and the points indicated have been chosen arbitrarily.*

Offspring: 1 is a chromosomally unbalanced and presumably inviable zygote; 2 is normal, phenotypically and chromosomally; 3 is a chromosomally balanced, phenotypically normal carrier; he is chromosomally distinct and will produce the same types of gametes and offspring as the affected parent; 4 is a mongol like A. (Reprinted by permission of Professor Polani and Lancet from Lancet 2:721-724, 1960.)

ism in the next generation would depend upon the segregation behavior of the chromosomes and not on parental age. The normal karyotypes observed in the parents of the patient indicated that in this particular case the translocation had arisen de novo. However, later in the same year, two families were reported, in each of which the translocation was found in a normal parent of a mongol as predicted.

Penrose *et al.* (27), described a family in which mongolism occurred in two sibs of opposite sex. In addition, there was one normal female sib and two miscarriages. Both mongols possessed the 13–15/21 translocation described above. The father had a normal complement. However, the normal sib, the mother, and the maternal grandmother were found to have only 45 chromosomes. There were only three bodies in the 21–22 group, instead of the four which would be expected in normal females, and five in the 13–15 group. In addition, there was the 13–15/21 translocated chromosome.

Carter *et al.* (6), reported a family in which the index patient was a typical mongol born when his mother was 22 years of age. There were two male sibs: one mongol who died at age five months and a normal male. In addition, there was a male first cousin who was diagnosed as a mongol and who died at age five hours. The patient was found to have a 13–15/21 translocation. His mother and maternal aunt (the mother of the cousin referred to previously) and the maternal grandmother also carried the translocation.

Since these early reports, many families in which this type of translocation occurs have been recorded (15, 31).

In the same communication in which they reported the occurrence of the 13–15/21 translocation, Penrose, *et al.* (27), discussed a male mongol with another form of translocation. The chromosome count was 46 and analysis showed only four bodies in the 21–22 + Y group and five in the 19–20 group. This was interpreted as a 21–22/21 translocation. Both parents had a normal karyotype.

Hamerton *et al.* (16), reported a family in which mongolism occurred in two sibs of opposite sex, both of whom were dead. However, the mother of these children was found to carry this 22/21 type of translocation.

Additional instances of this translocation have been reported since, but it appears to be more rare than the 13–15/21 translocation.

Instances of three other types of translocation associated with mongolism are known to the authors. The first of these, reported by Zellweger, *et al.* (40), involved an unusual variant of the 22/21 translocation. The second instance (3) was a translocation involving the #21 chromosome and the long arm of chromosome #2. This 2/21 translocation was observed in a normal man who had one mongol child not available for study. The father had two stem lines in cultures of leukocytes of peripheral blood. One cell line contained 45 chromosomes and the translocation just described, and the other a normal complement. Thus, he was a mosaic.

The third case was observed in our laboratory. The patient was a male born when his mother was 27 years old and his father 35. Chromosome analysis of blood cultures showed 47 chromosomes with 5 members in the 21–22 + Y group and 7 in the 13–15 group (Figure 6). The clinical diagnosis was definitely not that of the so-called D_1 syndrome (32). In addition, one of the #2 chromosomes had a short short arm. It is our interpretation that the extra body in the 13–15 group resulted from a reciprocal translocation involving the long arm of a #21 and the short arm of a #2 chromosome. Chromosome studies were carried out on the close relatives of the patient. The father and two of the sibs had a normal complement. However, the mother, maternal grandmother, and remaining two sibs carried the abnormal chromosome observed in the patient (Figure 7).

In a somewhat different category are the two peculiar cases of Fraccaro *et al.* (13), and Hamerton *et al.* (16). The first patient, an only child, was a male with 46 chromosomes. There were only four members in the 21–22 + Y group and five in the 19–20 group. This finding can be interpreted as a 21/22 translocation described above or as an isochromosome of the long arm of chromosome #21. The mother had a normal karyotype. Cytological analysis of skin cultures of the phenotypically normal father showed 47 chromosomes with an extra body in the 19–20 group. Later studies on peripheral blood cultures indicated a normal karyotype and thus it appeared that the father was a mosaic. The second patient, a male, had one sib, a mongol who was dead at the time of study. In addition, there had been one miscarriage reported. Cytological analysis of cells from two peripheral blood cultures showed that the patient was a mosaic. The large majority of cells had 46 chromosomes while a

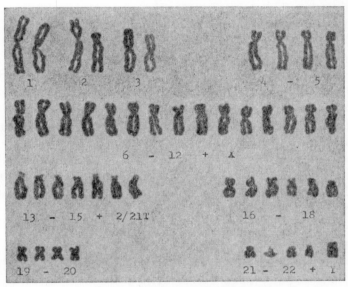

FIGURE 6. *Karyotype of a male mongol with the 2/21 translocation. There are only five 21–22 + Y chromosomes, but seven 13–15 chromosomes. The extra 13–15 chromosome is a 21 with part of the short arm of one of the #2 chromosomes attached.*

few had 47. The cells with 46 chromosomes had 5 bodies in the 19–20 group and only 3 in the 21–22 group. The cells with 47 chromosomes had 5 members in the 19–20 group and 4 in the 21–22 group. The mother had a normal karyotype. The majority of the father's cells had a normal complement but there were a few cells with 47 chromosomes. In the latter the karyotype was identical with that observed in the 47 cell line in the patient. Thus the patient and his father were mosaics. It is not feasible in this presentation to delve into the interpretation of these findings and the mechanisms by which such chromosomal structures arise. However, those readers interested in these aspects are referred to Hamerton's excellent discussion (15).

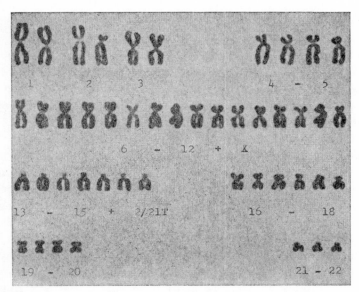

FIGURE 7. *Karyotype of a female 2/21 translocation carrier. Only three 21–22 group chromosomes are present, and there are seven 13–15 chromosomes. One of the #2 chromosomes has a short short arm.*

Mosaicism

In 1961, Clarke *et al.* (8) reported a case of a child with certain physical stigmata of mongolism—notably a mongoloid facies and characteristic palmar dermatoglyphics. Her I.Q. was 100 at age two years and three months. Cytological studies of skin and blood cultures showed a consistent mixture of two cell types, one with 46 and the other with 47 chromosomes. The cells with 46 bodies had a normal female karyotype, while those with 47 were trisomic for chromosome #21. As has already been stated, such a situation is known as mosaicism.

Before considering the significance of these chromosome aberrations in a proper understanding of mongolism it seems appropriate to discuss the mechanisms by which they arise.

CHROMOSOMAL MECHANISMS AND THE ORIGIN OF ABERRATIONS ASSOCIATED WITH MONGOLISM

The purpose of this section is to give a summary of the basic cytological mechanisms which relate directly to an understanding of the cytogenetics of mongolism. Readers are referred to basic cytology, cytogenetics, and genetics textbooks for a more complete discussion of this subject (34, 35).

Complement of the Normal Cell

The diploid or somatic number refers to the chromosome complement of the somatic cells, whereas the haploid or gametic number refers to the complement of the egg or sperm. There is a wide range of chromosome numbers in different species of plants and animals but the number in any one species is usually constant.

In normal human somatic cells there are 22 pairs of autosomal chromosomes and one pair of sex chromosomes, making the total somatic number 46. Cells of males have one X and a Y chromosome (XY), while the cells of females have two X chromosomes (XX). Autosomal pair members are called homologous chromosomes and each haploid or gametic set of chromosomes contains one member of a pair of homologs. Structurally normal homologous chromosomes are similar in all respects except that different allelic combinations are present in each one. The X and Y sex chromosomes differ markedly in morphology and have little or no homology.

Chromosome morphology varies from one stage of cell division to another. In this presentation only the morphology of the chromosomes at the metaphase stage of mitosis will be discussed. Human chromosomes are most often studied during this stage when the chromosomes are contracted and can be seen as distinct bodies. Each chromosome at somatic metaphase has a definite shape and relative length that are constant from cell to cell. The shape of the chromosome is determined by the position of the centromere or spindle fiber attachment. This is usually evident as a constriction in the chromosome at some definite point. The centromere may be near one end (e.g., groups 13–15 and 21–22 + Y in Figure 2), at the midpoint (e.g., groups 1–3 and 19–20 in Figure 2), or between the midpoint and the end of the chromosome (e.g., groups 4–5 and 6–12 + X and 16–18 in Figure 2). These chromosome types are termed *acrocentric*, *metacentric*, and *submetacentric*, respectively.

On some chromosomes, points other than the centromere are constricted. These secondary constrictions often pinch off a very small portion called a *satellite*. In man there are five pairs of satellited chromosomes (13–15 and 21–22) but the satellites are evident only in well-prepared material. In general, secondary constrictions and satellites are helpful landmarks in identifying particular chromosomes.

Although it varies from cell to cell in prepared material, the "genic" size of each chromosome is always constant. The observed length of a chromosome is determined by the amount of contraction that has taken place, thus absolute measurements of chromosomes cannot be made. Measurements of individual chromosomes must be evaluated as a ratio of the total length of all the chromosomes in the cell. Human chromosomes are classified on the basis of relative size and the position of the centromere (the arm ratio). Only within groups 1–3 and 16–18 of the seven distinct groups of chromosomes in the normal human complement can reasonably accurate identification of individual chromosomes and pairing of homologous chromosomes be made. Within the other five groups the morphologic similarity of the chromosomes makes accurate identification impossible.

Abnormal Chromosome Complements

Errors in cell division may lead to numerical changes in the chromosome complement. There are two kinds of cell division: *mitosis*, or somatic division, during which two daughter cells with identical chromosome complements are produced; and *meiosis*, during which gametes with one-half the normal somatic complement of chromosomes are produced.

Other mechanisms may produce structural alterations in the chromosomes. These altered forms may be modified or removed by the meiotic or mitotic processes.

NUMERICAL. The most common chromosomal errors found in man involve whole chromosomes. Such errors can be classified generally into two types: *euploidy,* in which the number of chromosomes is a mutiple of the haploid number (e.g., triploid, tetraploid, etc.); and *aneuploidy,* in which the number of chromosomes is not an even multiple of the haploid number. Only the latter type is pertinent to a discussion of mongolism.

Normally each chromosome is represented twice in the diploid complement. In aneuploid complements a chromosome may be represented by more or less than two members. A cell with three members of one chromosome is said to be trisomic for that chromosome. Cells may also be monosomic or tetrasomic for specific chromosomes. The unbalanced state caused by the presence of an extra chromosome or by the loss of a chromosome usually manifests itself in a specific aneuploid phenotype. The phenotype of mongolism is caused in most instances by the presence of chromosome #21 in triplicate.

The trisomic condition is thought to be caused by nondisjunction of chromosomes during cell division. The term *nondisjunction* means that chromosomes or chromatids (chromosomes in the first division of meiosis and chromatids in the second division of meiosis or in mitosis) which normally segregate during division fail to do so. This failure to segregate results in the inclusion of segregation partners in the same daughter cell.

Nondisjunction which occurs in the gonads of a person with a normal complement is termed *primary nondisjunction,* while that which occurs in individuals with a trisomy formed by previous nondisjunction is called *secondary nondisjunction.* This latter phenomenon has been found in some rare cases of familial mongolism and explains instances in which female mongols or normal individuals with gonadal mosaicism have given birth to mongols.

When nondisjunction occurs during spermatogenesis both types of abnormal gametes are produced, i.e., those with an extra chromosome and those lacking a chromosome. In oögenesis only one abnormal type of gamete is produced because one of the abnormal cells is lost as a polar body. A gamete with an extra chromosome, when united with a normal gamete, results in an individual trisomic for that chromosome; whereas a gamete lacking a chromosome will result in an individual monosomic for that chromosome. In man only the X chromosome has been found in the monosomic form. Apparently a monosomic condition of any of the autosomes is lethal. Trisomic states appear to be more compatible with life since trisomies of three autosomes and partial trisomies (those associated with reciprocal translocations) of many others have been observed.

Mitotic nondisjunction is the mechanism underlying the production of mosaic individuals. When nondisjunction occurs in the zygote or early embryo, one or more new cell lines may arise. If the abnormal division occurs very early in development (e.g., at the two- or four-cell stage) the new cell lines may constitute a major part of the cellular material of the mature individual. However, if the nondisjunction occurs later the new cell lines may represent only a minor part of the cellular makeup of the mature individual and, in fact, may be restricted to a single tissue. Many varieties of complex mosaicism can arise, depending upon the stage of development at which the anomalous division occurs and the viability of the products.

STRUCTURAL (INTERCHANGES, INTRACHANGES, AND ISOCHROMOSOMES). Interchanges and intrachanges arise initially from breakages in the chromosome arms and subsequent anomalous reunion of broken ends. The mechanisms underlying the breakage of chromosomes, which may occur both spontaneously and by experimental means, are subject to intense research at this time. Two main types of structural interchange and intrachange, namely, reciprocal translocations and inversions, are pertinent to a discussion of mongolism.

The broken ends of chromosomes are unstable and tend to unite with other broken ends. If the ends reunite to form the chromosome as it was before breakage, restitution is said to have taken place. If restitution does not occur, then a structural aberration will arise. It should be noted that intact chromosome ends or telomeres have the specific property of not entering into permanent association with other intact ends or broken ends.

If more than one break is present in a cell at the same time, the broken ends may reunite in an anomalous manner. The changes that result will depend upon whether the breaks are in the same or in different chromosomes. If the breaks occur in different chromosomes, either one of two types of reciprocal translocation may be produced. A symmetric or balanced translocation will result if each acentric fragment is translocated to a different centric fragment (Figure 8). At mitosis the interchange chromosomes will behave as normal chromosomes and will be passed on to the daughter cells. It is pertinent here to refer to the 13–15/21 and the 22/21 translocations associated in some instances with mongolism. These translocations are presumed to have originated as a balanced reciprocal type, but the small fusion product of the short arms is always lost, causing a deletion of parts of the two participating chromosomes. Thus, the "carrier" relatives have 45 chromosomes. The aberration acts like a balanced system, however, and these "carriers" are phenotypically normal (Figure 5).

The interchange is asymmetric if the two acentric fragments unite and the two centric fragments unite (Figure 8). At mitosis the acentric fusion product will be lost and the dicentric will probably be broken. Cells with such interchanges are usually not viable and asymmetric translocations are not found as aberrations in man.

If two breaks occur in the same chromosome, then a section of the chromosome may be inverted. The inversion is pericentric if the centromere is included in the inverted region and paracentric if the centromere is excluded. A paracentric inversion does not alter visibly the somatic metaphase morphology of the chromosome and can be discovered only by genetic evidence and certain cytologic observations. However, a pericentric inversion, if asymmetric about the centromere, will change the morphology of the somatic metaphase chromosome. A pericentric inversion in a maternal chromosome #21 was thought to be implicated in the production of a mongol in one family (14).

Finally, some mention should be made of isochromosomes which result when the centromere divides transversely rather than longi-

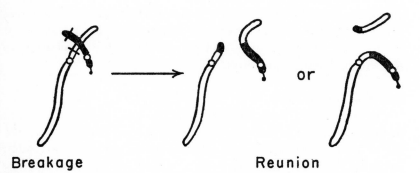

Breakage **Reunion**

FIGURE 8. *Chromosome breakage followed by reunion of ends to form a symmetrical reciprocal translocation or an asymmetrical reciprocal translocation.*

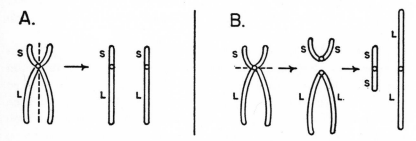

FIGURE 9. *Isochromosome formation. (A) Normal division of the centromere. (B) Transverse division of the centromere forming two isochromosomes.*

tudinally in mitosis. The long arms are separated from the short arms of the chromosome, producing two metacentric chromosomes each with two genetically identical arms (Figure 9). The daughter cell receiving only one of these chromosomes would have a duplication of one arm of the original chromosome and a deficiency of the other. The formation of an isochromosome is a rare event.

USE OF CYTOGENETIC KNOWLEDGE IN CLINICAL
PRACTICE: PREVENTIVE MEASURES
AND GENETIC COUNSELING

Cytogenetic studies are of limited value in diagnosing mongolism since the vast majority of cases can be diagnosed at birth or shortly afterward by a thorough routine physical examination. Their real value is in obtaining a better understanding of the fundamental mechanisms of the disease and in utilizing this knowledge to institute preventive measures.

Maternal Age Dependency

The number of mongols born in Caucasian populations could be reduced by one-half if women stopped having children after the age of 35. The largest group of mongols by cytogenetic classification comprises the #21 trisomics which appear to be maternal age dependent. Therefore, the problem is to seek the basis for the association of nondisjunction and increasing maternal age. This is far from clear at the present time, but theories on the subject have been discussed by Hamerton (15). It is obvious that the final answer resides in a better understanding of human oögenesis, which is an extremely difficult process to study.

There is evidence from the work of Uchida and Curtis (37) that women who give birth to mongols have a history of radiation exposure which is much greater than that experienced by women who give birth to nonmongols. Although this work has not been confirmed, it suggests that a woman who has been exposed to high levels of radiation might have an increased risk of giving birth to a mongol in her later reproductive years. Further work is needed to confirm this finding and to seek other factors which might have a similar influence. It should be stressed that these factors must fit within the framework of our knowledge of human oögenesis and the mechanism of nondisjunction.

Therefore, since the most common type of mongolism can be anticipated only by its association with advancing maternal age, prevention, at present, rests on cautioning women of the risk they run as they approach their later reproductive years.

Familial Mongolism

Two situations exist in which a high risk of mongolism occurs. The first is in the subsequent pregnancies of a relatively young woman who has already given birth to a mongol. The second is in families in which two or more cases of mongolism have already occurred. In both instances, cytogenetic studies can be of value in determining if the high-risk situation obtains or not.

THE YOUNG MOTHER. A young woman with a mongol child is naturally concerned about the defect recurring in subsequent offspring. Chromosome studies are indicated in such a situation. In the vast majority of cases, the trisomy for #21 will be observed and the woman can be informed that the risk of recurrence is slight (Table I). However, she should be cautioned about the increased risk after the age of 35.

TABLE I. *Occurrence and recurrence risk figures for mongolism by maternal age*

Maternal Age	Percent Risk	Percent Recurrence Risk
15–19	0.05	2.5–3.0
20–24	0.06	2.5–3.0
25–29	0.07	0.5
30–34	0.12	0.5
35–39	0.38	1.0–2.0
40–44	1.07	1.0–2.0
45 +	1.86	1.0–2.0

If a translocation is observed in the patient, chromosome studies should be carried out on the parents. If the translocation is found, close relatives of the "carrier" parent should be studied as well.

FAMILIES WITH RECURRENCE. Individuals in families in which mongolism has already recurred are concerned about the risk which they run of transmitting the defect to their offspring. In such situations, the most efficient way of approaching the problem is to examine the chromosomes of the mongols who are still living. If a translocation is present, then a search for the "carrier" state in all close relatives is indicated. If the mongolism proves to be of the trisomic variety, two interpretations are possible.

First, a gene for nondisjunction may be segregating in the family. In such situations the risk of occurrence in the offspring of a normal relative is probably increased over the risk that is given in Table I. Genes for nondisjunction are known in *Drosophila,* and families in which mongolism and Klinefelter's syndrome occur in the same sibship are probably good evidence that such genes also exist in man.

The second interpretation might be that one of the parents, in cases of recurrence among sibs, is a mosaic. If the mosaicism occurs in both somatic and germinal tissues, then it may be detected by chromosome studies. If it is confined to the germinal tissue, i.e., gonadal mosaicism, it will not be evident in the cultures of somatic tissues. Penrose (26) has indicated that as many as 10 percent of the mothers of mongols may be mosaics and that this mosaicism can be detected by the dermatoglyphic microsymptoms mentioned previously. If this proves to be the case, then it might be advisable eventually to study the dermatoglyphics of all young women giving birth to a mongol with trisomy #21, regardless of whether the defect has already occurred in the immediate family.

Risk figures for the counseling of parents of mongols about recurrence in subsequent offspring are presented in Table I. These estimates are derived from data presented by Carter and Evans (7) and probably are valid for most Caucasian populations. It is seen that the recurrence risk figures for the younger maternal age groups are markedly elevated over the population risk for that age group. This presumably reflects the bias imposed by the high-risk situations of familial mongolism—genes for nondisjunction, translocations, and mosaicism.

In these situations the theoretical recurrence risk may be extremely high (in the order of 30–50 percent), but it is very difficult to test the theory because of gross deficiencies in our knowledge of fundamental processes in human cytogenetics. For example, since the existence in man of genes for nondisjunction is a matter of speculation, little can be done aside from warning parents of the possible increased risk. In the case of parental mosaicism, the problem resides in our inability to measure its exact extent and nature. For example, if the dichotomy is an extreme one, dividing the normal somatic tissue from trisomic germinal tissue, then the risk would be in the order of 50 percent, i.e., the same as it appears to be for the offspring of mongols themselves. It is highly unlikely that such a sharp division ever exists and it is more likely that the germinal tissue would contain both normal and trisomic cells. However, it is difficult to specify an exact risk figure and all that is possible is a general indication that the risk is somewhat higher than the figures in Table I.

Cases of translocation provide the most promising situation for concrete counseling advice. Unfortunately, this counseling must be based largely on empiric data rather than a theoretical consideration of meiotic segregation behavior of complements containing translocations. Analysis to date of pedigrees in which translocations are segregating seems to indicate that carriers are more prevalent than either mongols or normal noncarriers. Although both sexes may carry the translocation, females seem to transmit it more than males. The 22/21 translocation may be an exception to this rule since at present there appears to be a paternal effect in the small number of families reported to date (25). From present data, it appears that female carriers with the translocation have approximately a 20 percent risk of having a mongol (41). It should be stressed that this is an empiric risk figure and each pedigree should be analyzed on its own merits before counseling advice is given.

FUTURE INVESTIGATIONS

On the basis of purely theoretical genetic considerations, it is reasonable to expect that the various chromosomal types of mongolism should be distinguishable on clinical grounds. Gene function is a product of its environment and therefore one would not expect a trisomic state to present exactly the same phenotype as a translocation state. In a similar manner, the "normal carriers" of a translocation should show some clinical evidence of this state. Penrose's earlier observations on familial mongolism and microsymptoms in normal relatives have been brought up to date and correlated with carriers of translocations and mosaicism and it now appears that certain dermatoglyphic patterns may be sensitive indicators of the presence of these carrier states (25). It would seem reasonable to believe that additional morphologic and metabolic indicators exist which would prove of value in this regard.

The association of the Philadelphia chromosome (Ph¹) with granulocytic leukemia (21) and its possible relation to the frequent occurrence of leukemia in mongols may ultimately lead to the genetic mapping of chromosome #21. This, in turn, may eventually lead to an understanding of the metabolic action of this chromosome which results in the production of the mongol phenotype.

At present, preventive measures in mongolism are based on empiric data. It seems reasonable to expect that development of our knowledge of basic cytological mechanisms in man will lead to more reliable occurrence and recurrence risk figures and hence to sounder preventive procedures.

REFERENCES

1. Allen, G., and Baroff, G. S. Mongoloid twins and their siblings. *Acta Genet.* (Basel) 5:294-326, 1955.
2. Barr, M. L., and Bertram, E. G. A morphological distinction between neurones of the male and female, and the behavior of the nucleolar satellite during accelerated nucleoprotein synthesis. *Nature* (London) 163:676-677, 1949.
3. Becker, K. L., and Albert, A. Familial translocation mongolism: A carrier exhibiting nonacrocentric translocation. *Proc. Mayo Clin.* 38:261-267, 1963.
4. Böök, J. A., Fraccaro, M., and Lindstrom, J. Cytogenetical observations in mongolism. *Acta Paediat.* (Uppsala) 48:453-468, 1959.
5. Brothwell, D. R. A possible case of mongolism in a Saxon population. *Ann. Hum. Genet.* 24:141-150, 1960.

6. Carter, C. O., Hamerton, J. L., Polani, P. E., Gunalp, A., and Weller, S. D. Chromosome translocation as a cause of familial mongolism. *Lancet* 2:678-680, 1960.

7. Carter, C. O., and Evans, K. A. Risk of parents who have had one child with Down's syndrome (mongolism) having another child similarly affected. *Lancet* 2:785-788, 1961.

8. Clarke, C. M., Edwards, J. H., and Smallpiece, V. 21-Trisomy/ normal mosaicism. *Lancet* 1:1028-1030, 1961.

9. Cohen, B. H., Lilienfeld, A. M., and Sigler, A. T. Some epidemiological aspects of mongolism: A review. *Amer. J. Public Health* 53:223-236, 1963.

10. Collman, R. D., and Stoller, A. A survey of mongoloid births in Victoria, Australia, 1942-1957. *Amer. J. Public Health* 52:813-829, 1962.

11. Down, J. L. H. Observations on an ethnic classification of idiots. *London Hosp. Rep.* 3:259-262, 1866.

12. Ford, C. E., *et al.* The chromosomes in a patient showing both mongolism and the Klinefelter syndrome. *Lancet* 1:709-710, 1959.

13. Fraccaro, M., Kaijser, K., and Lindsten, J. Chromosomal abnormalities in father and mongol child. *Lancet* 1:724-727, 1960.

14. Gray, J. E., Mutlow, D. E., and Ashby, D. W. Pericentric inversion of chromosome 21. A possible further cytogenetic mechanism in mongolism. *Lancet* 1:21-23, 1962.

15. Hamerton, J. L. Cytogenetics of Mongolism. In J. L. Hamerton (ed.), *Chromosomes in Medicine.* Little Club Clinic Dev. Med. 5. London: National Spastics Society and Heinemann Medical Books, 1962.

16. Hamerton, J. L., Briggs, S. M., Gianelli, F., and Carter, C. O. Chromosome studies in the selection of parents with a high risk of a second mongol child. *Lancet* 2:788-791, 1961.

17. Jacobs, P. A., Baikie, A. G., Court Brown, W. M., and Strong, J. A. The somatic chromosomes in mongolism. *Lancet* 1:710, 1959.

18. Jenkins, R. L. Etiology of mongolism. *Amer. J. Dis. Child.* 45:506-519, 1933.

19. Lejeune, J., Gautier, M., and Turpin, R. Étude des chromosomes somatiques de neuf enfants mongoliens. *C. R. Acad. Sci.* (Paris) 248:1721-1722, 1959.

20. McKusick, V. A. Medical genetics 1961. *J. Chronic Dis.* 15:417-572, 1962.

21. Nowell, P. C., and Hungerford, D. A. A minute chromosome

in human chronic granulocytic leukemia. *Science* 132:1497, 1960.

22. Penrose, L. S. The relative aetiological importance of birth order and maternal age in mongolism. *Proc. Roy. Soc. Biol.* 115:431-450, 1934.

23. Penrose, L. S. Maternal age in familial mongolism. *J. Ment. Sci.* 97:738-747, 1951.

24. Penrose, L. S. Mongolism. *Brit. Med. Bull.* 17:184-189, 1961.

25. Penrose, L. S. Paternal age in mongolism. *Lancet* 1:1101, 1962.

26. Penrose, L. S. Dermatoglyphs in mosaic mongolism and allied conditions. *Proc. XI Int. Cong. Genetics* 3:973-980, 1965.

27. Penrose, L. S., Ellis, J. R., and Delhanty, J. D. A. Chromosomal translocations in mongolism and in relatives. *Lancet* 2:409-410, 1960.

28. Polani P. E., *et al.* A mongol girl with 46 chromosomes. *Lancet* 2:721-724, 1960.

29. Renwick, G. R., Miller, J. R., and Paterson, D. R. Estimates of incidence and prevalence of mongolism and of congenital heart disease in British Columbia. *Canad. Med. Assoc. J.* 91:365-371, 1964.

30. Report of a study group: A proposed standard system on nomenclature of human mitotic chromosomes. *Amer. J. Hum. Genet.* 12:384-388, 1960.

31. Shaw, M. W. Familial mongolism. *Cytogenetics* 1:141-179, 1962.

32. Smith, D. W., *et al.* The D_1 trisomy syndrome. *J. Pediat.* 62:326-341, 1963.

33. Stern, C. The chromosomes of man. *Amer. J. Hum. Genet.* 11:301-314, 1959.

34. Stern, C. *Principles of Human Genetics* (2nd ed.). San Francisco: Freeman, 1960.

35. Swanson, C. P. *Cytology and Cytogenetics.* Englewood Cliffs, N.J.: Prentice-Hall, 1957.

36. Tjio, J. H., and Levan, A. The chromosome number of man. *Hereditas* (Lund) 42:1-6, 1956.

37. Uchida, I. A., and Curtis, E. J. A possible association between maternal radiation and mongolism. *Lancet* 2:848-850, 1961.

38. Waardenburg, P. L. *Das menschliche Auge und seine Erbanlangen.* The Hague: Martinus Nijhoff, 1932.

39. Warkany, J. Etiology of mongolism. *J. Pediat.* 56:412-419, 1960.

40. Zellweger, H., Mikamo, K., and Abbo, G. An unusual translocation in a case of mongolism. *J. Pediat.* 62:225-229, 1963.

41. Zellweger, H. Familial mongolism: History and present status. *Clin. Pediat.* 3:291-303, 1964.

Development of a Child Psychiatry Service in a Pediatric or General Hospital

DENIS LAZURE

HISTORICAL NOTE

During the early decades of this century, interest became focused at first on two aspects of disturbed child life: the child disturbed in social behavior and the child presenting an educational problem because of personality disturbances.

As time passed and knowledge of adult neurosis increased, it became apparent that this adult affliction was in part rooted in the mental ill health of the child. Thus, interest was now focused on the mental health of the child and on his psychological development. Clinical entities with defined psychopathology and/or organic pathology became recognized, and the clinical nature of these problems was reflected in the setting up of child psychiatry or child guidance clinics by the health services or by voluntary bodies. The number of these clinics has rapidly increased in recent years but, in North America, we only now begin to detect a definite tendency to develop these clinics as part of a hospital, preferably a pediatric hospital or a general hospital which has a large pediatric department (e.g., a university medical center), and sometimes as part of an existing psychiatric hospital for adults or as an addition to a hospital school for retarded children.

Until 15 years ago, most psychiatric facilities for children consisted of outpatient clinics in which the most common form of treatment was the weekly psychotherapeutic session for the child and the weekly casework interview for the parent. Diagnostic procedures were generally limited to the psychiatric or psychological assessment of the child and to the social history of the family.

The rapprochement between child psychiatry and the pediatric or general hospital has had a number of significant consequences:

1. It allows for a more complete range of psychiatric services to the children: e.g., day care and treatment can be more easily carried out within a service that has an inpatient unit.

2. The constant availability of the medical consultants and of the diagnostic tools of the hospital ensures a more thorough assessment of conditions which have a mixed etiology (i.e., organic and psychologic), such as mental retardation, psychomotor instability associated with brain damage, and psychosomatic disorders.

3. The child psychiatrist remains in contact with his medical colleagues and his daily presence in the hospital facilitates the integration of psychiatry with other branches of medicine as applied to the child. Teaching thus gains an impetus at all levels: medical students, interns, and residents in pediatrics become exposed not only to the principles of mental health and the psychiatric syndromes in the child but also to the specific contributions of the other professions within the child psychiatry team.

4. The presence of child psychiatry as one of the services of the hospital promotes the awareness of the medical staff vis-à-vis the psychiatric symptoms in their patients and results in early detection and referral.

5. Research is considerably enlarged in its scope and enriched by the stimulating interest of scientists with diversified types of training.

It has taken child psychiatry a much longer time to enter into the pediatric hospital or department than it did for adult psychiatry to enter into the general hospital, and perhaps the development of child guidance clinics geographically and otherwise dissociated from the hospitals has largely contributed to this lag. Naturally, in this process of integration with other medical services of the hospital, child psychiatry is encountering the resistance that faced general psychiatrists some twenty years ago.

However, it is now recognized that: (1) a well-organized child psychiatry service is an essential part of any modern pediatric hospital; (2) a university hospital is not a complete entity if it has no child psychiatry service; and (3) any general hospital that has an important pediatrics department should seriously consider creating such a service in close association with that department and with the department of psychiatry (8, 13).

And yet, in these three types of hospitals, the actual setting up of a well-organized and complete child psychiatry service is not taking place rapidly enough. For example, only two cities (Montreal and Edmonton) in the whole of Canada, have thus far succeeded in organizing such a service; although a few other cities (Toronto, Vancouver, Winnipeg) are well advanced in their planning stage (11).

FUNCTIONS OF A CHILD
PSYCHIATRY SERVICE

Whatever the administrative background, a psychiatric service for children exists to serve the community by providing for the investigation, diagnosis, and treatment of children and adolescents whose departures from mental health are manifest as psychological symptoms, somatic symptoms, disturbed habit formation, and disturbances in personal relationships, social conduct or adaptation to education.

Such symptoms may be related to genetic or intercurrent handicapping in the physical, intellectual, or emotional aspects of the individual; they are most commonly reactive to environmental stress in the relationships within the family. Less commonly, they may be reactive to demands inappropriate to the capacities and needs of the child at school or at work. However determined, the symptoms represent the child's attempted solution to his inborn needs and developmental goals in the face of personal limitations or environmental stress (6).

The symptoms may range in severity from mild reactive symptoms to neurotic or psychotic illnesses. The syndrome may occasionally be one largely determined by psychological anomaly or organic damage.

These facts underline the continuity of the practice of child psychiatry with that of adult psychiatry and other medical specialties, especially pediatrics and neurology. The child psychiatric service aims to restore the child's mental health and to forestall adult mental ill health. By outlining the conditions necessary for mental health in the child, the service has an important preventive function. The pediatric or general hospital needs a psychiatric staff to help in the evaluation, diagnosis, and treatment of emotional complications, which, for the most part, can be managed in the medical, surgical, and pediatric services. The child psychiatrist, giving advice and supervision, can help physician and nurses gain better understanding of their young patients and thus provide more effective treatment.

Because such a hospital is well integrated into most communities, there is usually less disruption of the child's life than there would be if he became a patient in a psychiatric hospital. Moreover, continuity of treatment is usually possible when it is conducted in the community hospital. The child may have the continued services of his pediatrician or family doctor, thus not having to break off his relationship with his physician just when he most urgently needs it.

Whenever possible, diagnostic and treatment services should be administered in outpatient or day care facilities in order to avoid traumatic reactions which are sometimes caused by separation from the family and to foster the close involvement of the parents in the therapeutic process. Even when necessary, hospitalization must be viewed as a phase of the treatment which can be considerably reduced if further emphasis is placed upon extending outpatient and community treatment. Incidentally, the child psychiatrist, through his teaching and consultation work, is in a favorable position to draw the attention of his medical colleagues to the noxious effects on the child's psyche of unnecessary or unduly prolonged hospitalization.

Other basic functions of the child psychiatry service include teaching, training, and research. Again, those functions are best carried out if the service is part of a pediatric or general hospital, since such an institution already has a tradition and an active program, often university-sponsored, in the three areas (12).

NEED FOR A CHILD PSYCHIATRY SERVICE

Because there are so few systematic epidemiological studies of psychiatric disturbances in children, it is difficult to arrive at a precise estimate of the needs for child psychiatric services. Findings regarding the incidence of mental retardation appear to coincide in most Western countries and it is generally agreed that at least 3 percent of the child population suffers from some degree of mental deficiency and will thus require at least psychiatric diagnostic services.

Antisocial behavior, insofar as it brings the youth into the hands of the law, can also be measured fairly accurately through juvenile court statistics. Thus, at any given time in the United States, 5 percent of the population below the age of 18 is officially considered juvenile delinquent. It is reasonable to assume that for the large majority of these children, diagnostic and treatment facilities are necessary.

Other types of maladjustment including neurotic and psychotic disorders are much more difficult to assess as to their incidence: depending on the studies, statistics vary from 8 to 20 percent of the school-age population (14).

British health and education authorities have adopted the following as a minimum norm for the needs of child psychiatric services in their country: 1 outpatient clinic (consisting of 1 child psychiatrist, 2 psychologists, and 3 social workers) per 45,000 school children, and a minimum of 40 beds (excluding mentally defectives) for a general population of 500,000 (3). However, experts in the United States feel that a one-team clinic (1 psychiatrist, 1 psychologist, and 1 social worker) per population (general) of 50,000 is a minimum. Child psychiatrists in Sweden, Denmark, and Finland share the same opinion, based on several epidemiological surveys which all concur to show that 15 percent of the children are in need of psychiatric attention; and from our own experience we have also come to fully endorse this opinion (10).

There can be no rigid rule in percentage or otherwise as to how the psychiatric beds or clinics should be distributed. However, it should be obvious that a pediatric hospital does not correspond to current standards if it does not have a structured and complete child psychiatry service with a number of beds varying between 5 and 10 percent of the total bed capacity of the hospital. A general hospital with a large pediatric department should have a small inpatient psychiatric unit (approximately 10 beds) and, of course, a child psychiatry outpatient clinic: this is an even more important requisite if such a general hospital is part of a university medical center (8). Hospitalization of a child in the psychiatry service is less often indicated than it is for the adult patient; and if a child psychiatry service has an active outpatient clinic as well as a thorough program for day patients, the number of cases where hospitalization is essential can be surprisingly reduced. Hence, the proposed figure is 5–10 percent of the total bed capacity of the hospital as compared with the 10–15 percent which is advocated in adult psychiatry.

CLINICAL STRUCTURE

Any developing service eventually realizes the necessity of dividing its clinical services into semi-autonomous entities, each one having its director-psychiatrist and its professional team. The following structure has been found convenient within the framework of a large pediatric hospital: outpatient clinic, inpatient clinic, day care clinic, consultation clinic, mental assessment clinic and learning problems clinic. The six clinical directors are directly responsible to the chief of the service, with whom they meet regularly as a group in order to evaluate continuously the policy of each clinic and its specific role in the global functioning of the service.

A great deal of freedom is left to the director of each clinic in the daily decision-making and in the internal organization of his section. He and his collaborators form a homogeneous group which meets almost daily. The paramedical staff is assigned to one clinic for a year or more. This stability within a very circumscribed area and under close leadership, results in authentic teamwork. On the other hand, the weekly clinical conference for the total staff of the service permits scientific exchanges cutting across the boundaries of the clinics and permits the identification of the individual with the spirit and goals of the service as well as those of "his" clinic.

Outpatient Clinic

Within such a structure, the outpatient clinic remains the main pillar of the service. In addition to its own specific functions in regard to diagnosis and treatment, the outpatient clinic also acts as the coordinating agent for all the clinics. Except for the cases referred directly to the consultation clinic by the pediatric staff of the wards or of the outpatient clinics, all new patients (including those who may be hospitalized in the inpatient clinic) are registered in the outpatient clinic for the intake interview. On the basis of the information gathered, the director may decide that the diagnostic evaluation will be performed by the outpatient clinic team or he may immediately transfer the case to one of the other five special clinics. In the latter case, depending upon the findings of the assessment, it is possible that the patient may be referred back to the outpatient clinic if treatment does not have to be administered within one of the specialized clinics.

As it is well known, most of the outpatient clinics have at least one thing in common: the problem of dealing with a long waiting list, especially of cases for whom psychotherapy is prescribed. This phenomenon is caused by other factors in addition to the shortage of personnel in relation to ever-increasing demands in the community. It may be useful to reexamine some of the traditional attitudes and techniques prevalent among the staff, which may hinder the efficiency of the service.

It seems that the natural tendency of any treating person to view the patient as his "protégé" is considerably intensified when the patient is a child, with the result that the latter becomes "overpro-tected" and monopolized. Thus, even when a short-term therapy would be more beneficial than a protracted one, the therapist is often prone to maintain the treatment situation because of this loss of objectivity.

Treatment can also be unnecessarily prolonged when, in the thera-pist's scale of values, long-term and intensive therapy is given top priority, with the result that an alternative therapy is regarded as an insult to his principles or a threat to his self-esteem.

In services which have an important teaching program for resi-dents in psychiatry, it is common to find that most of the treatment of the children is performed by these young physicians in training while most of the psychiatrist's time is devoted to supervision and teaching. To a large extent this is inevitable. However, this trend, which was more necessary when there were fewer trained child psy-chiatrists, can now be utilized as a tradition and a rationalization on the part of the staff psychiatrists to avoid clinical work with the public outpatient cases and to take refuge in private practice.

The skill of the experienced staff psychiatrist should be used to develop new treatment techniques, either with one patient or with a group of children.

For example, it has proved useful to have a staff physician hold one or two half-day clinics to assess globally and quickly a number of urgent cases and to report the same day to the parents, while pre-senting them with concrete recommendations.

The experienced physician may also spend an equivalent amount of time in treating with atypical methods those children who may benefit from pharmacotherapy or from a depth therapy which does not have to be frequent.

One also wonders why group techniques are not more widely used in the treatment of children, since the group situation is more familiar and natural to the child than to the adult. Clinics which have had a good deal of experience with group therapy, especially if they have been flexible in offering diversified types of group therapy (conventional verbal therapy, psychodrama à la Moreno, analytic psychodrama, activity-therapy, play therapy, and combined play-verbal therapy) have reported results which compare favorably with individual therapy. A minor but interesting finding is that there is less absenteeism in children treated in groups as compared to those treated individually.

A seven-year experience shows that out of a large reservoir of children assigned for psychotherapy as outpatients, at least 50 percent will benefit greatly from group therapy.

Inpatient Clinic

The architectural organization of such a section obviously requires the consideration, among other things, of the following points: the philosophy underlying the therapeutic program, the types of psychiatric troubles under treatment, the number and ages of inpatient children; the duration of hospitalization, the organization and structure of the institution to which the section belongs (1, 2, 13).

LOCATION OF THE SECTION. The section should preferably be located on the ground floor so that the children may have direct access to an outside play area.

The section should be located in a quiet part of the hospital and a buffer zone should be provided between the part reserved for patients of the section and the remainder of the hospital.

DISTRIBUTION OF QUARTERS. It is not necessary that all the quarters of the section form a single unit on a single floor. On the contrary, there is some advantage in separating some quarters (rooms for physical activities, occupational therapy, classrooms). A certain dispersal could prevent the patients from living in confined spaces and would break the monotony and lonesomeness which result from constant habitation in the same quarters.

Sufficient space is needed to give a feeling of freedom. Different quarters are needed to create variety in the environment and quarters which lend themselves to the activities needed by children. Children in this section are not bedridden and so less accent is placed on the bedroom.

CONSTRUCTION OF QUARTERS. The selection of materials, the construction, and the furnishings should aim at providing safety, solidity, and usefulness. Special care should be given to sound-proofing especially in quarters where patients will have group activities. Decoration tries to create a pleasant environment and will make use of colors and materials suitable to the taste of the child.

DIVISION OF THE SECTION. The section should provide different units according to the age of the patients, the sex, and the reason for their hospitalization.

It is important that adolescents be placed in a unit separate from that of younger children. In general, it is preferable to organize separate units for adolescents of each sex, but a separation according to sex is not recommended for younger children. At any age it is also important to separate units organized for treatment from those organized for observation and diagnosis. Such divisions do not exclude the fact that certain quarters may be shared in common by one or several units.

The duration of the hospitalization in an observation unit may vary from two to eight weeks, extending from three to six months in the treatment units.

In a general manner, the observation units should offer greater safety and allow closer supervision by a larger staff. Treatment units should be organized to encourage a greater freedom for patients. Adolescents require more privacy than younger children.

The inpatient clinic should be reserved for children whose psychiatric or emotional disorders are so complex that their diagnosis or treatment, or both, are not possible either in an outpatient clinic, a day care clinic, or a pediatric ward.

Such a clinic, within a pediatric or general hospital, can perform its best services if it is geared to relatively short-term hospitalization, i.e., three to six weeks for most cases and as long as six months for exceptional cases where intensive treatment can only be administered in that living situation, either because of the child's or family's pathology or because of geographical reasons.

Brief separations from the family to allow the child to live for a while in a therapeutic milieu can bring dramatic improvement, especially if the family equilibrium has been destroyed because of acute neurotic interaction between the child and his parents or other members of the family, or both.

Whether the hospitalization is for assessment or for treatment, it is essential in most cases that the parents or their substitutes be available to the psychiatric team at least once a week during that period.

Various schools of thought exist as to what group of persons is best prepared and equipped to provide child care in an inpatient clinic: some clinics rely heavily on child-care workers, some on "special" educators, and others on nurses. We have been most happy with the latter group, especially when the nurses came either from pediatrics or from psychiatry; however, it is necessary to give an inservice training of one year in child psychiatric nursing. Male and female assistants should be taught theoretical and practical fundamentals in the techniques of observation and therapeutic attitudes.

At least half of the nursing staff should consist of nurses who have received the previously mentioned special training; and for a clinic which admits boys and girls, the nursing assistants who account for the other half should be predominantly male. The staff-patient ratio should be no less than 1:1, taking into account the usual work shifts of a hospital, the weekly and other holidays, and the absences for sickness.

In such a clinic open to children of both sexes below age 12, which accepts diagnostic as well as treatment cases, it would seem that the number of beds should be between 10 and 20. Below this minimum, it becomes uneconomical and also unsatisfactory for teaching, training, and research purposes. Furthermore, too small a number of patients limits the choice of peers too narrowly because of the wide range in the ages of the children.

It is important for most of the hospitalized children to maintain a daily contact with schoolwork when their condition allows it. Even more important, perhaps, is the role that a specialized teacher plays within the diagnostic team.

Day Care Clinic

In this clinical service, child psychiatry shows a lag as compared to "adult" psychiatry which has largely utilized day clinics or day hospitals for over ten years.

In many clinics for children, the demand and the need for a day program first became obvious with patients of preschool age; not only for the very disturbed psychotic or prepsychotic children in whom such a severe pathology appearing so early called for an intensive treatment, but also for the neurotic young child who is unable to attend a nursery school because of excessive fears, separation anxiety, and such, and yet seems to need more contact with a group. At the same time, for the mental health of the parents and the siblings, it is often necessary to remove the problem child from the home for at least one half of the day.

Thus, a day care clinic usually begins as a specialized nursery school and is often restricted to that level. This is unfortunate because many children of school age may need, for periods of days or weeks, this halfway status between the hospitalized patients and the one seen only weekly in the outpatient clinic.

This is true, for example, of the child who has had a rather long stay in the inpatient clinic and who can reintegrate his normal school environment only in a gradual fashion by spending several hours per week in the day clinic, or the child who presents a complex problem which can be better evaluated if observation can be carried out for a good part of the day without having to hospitalize him.

A day clinic operating within a complete service can, of course, make use of the facilities of the inpatient clinic so that, in addition to the psychiatric procedures of diagnosis and treatment, the child profits from a program consisting of remedial teaching, occupational therapy, and recreation activities.

Even if one includes the cost of a transportation system which soon becomes necessary in a day clinic, such a facility represents a sizable saving as compared with the cost of having the child as an inpatient.

Consultation Clinic

This clinic has a particular importance insofar as it acts as the link between the child psychiatry service and the other services of the hospital. Often, it is only through this clinic that the hospital staff will judge the quality of the service in general and the contribution that they feel child psychiatry is making to pediatrics.

It is obvious, therefore, that the staff responsible for consultation both in the hospital's wards and in the outpatient clinics must be acutely aware that it is being called upon to evaluate quickly and soundly someone else's patient and that results of the investigation have to be communicated to the treating physician in a language that cuts across the lines of the various medical specialties. Recommendations offered must be stated in a clear and yet not authoritative fashion. They must be concrete and realistic without being oversimplified.

The content of the consultation report must avoid doctrinaire or ambiguous statements which may, if used by the treating physician who reports to the parents, lend a meaning not intended by the psychiatrist or the psychologist.

In such a clinic, too, it is most important that the consultants of the various disciplines (psychiatrist, psychologist, social worker, and sometimes a teacher) should be assigned as a homogeneous team to one or several services in the hospital for a period of six months or more. Because the conditions for evaluation and treatment are less favorable than in the psychiatry service proper, it is essential that a senior staff be assigned to the consultation clinic.

Ideally, each consultation should be looked upon as an occasion for teaching as well as giving a service to a confrère and to the nursing staff. Paradoxically, a consultation clinic of high caliber in these two areas (service and teaching) should bring about an eventual decrease in the number of requests from pediatricians, who by then will have learned to cope with and treat some of the minor psychiatric problems.

This learning experience is especially appreciated by the pediatrician when the consultation takes place in the outdoor or emergency clinics, because he then has the opportunity to observe the psychiatrist's techniques, not only with the child but also with his parents. It has been our experience that a consultation team in such settings has proven to be an excellent investment of time, since among other results, it has greatly reduced the number of unnecessary or "unready" referrals to our outpatient clinic.

Mental Assessment Clinic

Children suspected of mental retardation are best assessed in a clinic that is part of a general hospital since so often the investigation will have to include the contribution of such fields as endocrinology, neurology, electroencephalography, genetics, and biochemistry.

To evaluate those children in such a specialized clinic, rather than in the regular outpatient clinic, has several advantages: (1) the diagnostic process differs from the one applied to the "psychiatric" case, some of the usual elements being superfluous and some more specific techniques being required; and (2) the clinical team develops special skills to interpret the child's condition to the parents and to deal with the often more acute but less prolonged problems of the defective child's parents as compared with the problems of the parents of an emotionally sick child. Such a team will also be continuously aware of the facilities to which the retarded child should be referred and finally it will gradually evolve special psychotherapeutic techniques (individual or collective) which will be needed for a minor proportion of those patients; pharmacotherapy will also be indicated in many cases.

In the past, child psychiatrists working usually within child guidance clinics have been accused of professional neglect toward the mentally retarded children. The criticism was justified to the extent that, not so long ago, many such clinics had admission policies which excluded the child with subnormal intelligence. Now that such exclusion is rarely seen, we must strive to train psychiatrists who will not only be willing to assess and help those children but who will also be equipped with the necessary competence. In this respect, the training acquired by the resident in the mental assessment clinic of a child psychiatry service, combined with the training received in hospitals and schools for the retarded, should give us some assurance that in the near future, a number of child psychiatrists will become true specialists in mental retardation.

Learning Problems Clinic

The names of Binet and Simon hold a place of honor in the history of child psychiatry, and the contribution of those two French scientists had a significant influence early in this century, in the development of child psychiatry. In their research with schoolchildren, Binet and Simon paid a good deal of attention to problems of learning. However, in the following decades, child psychiatry was much more concerned with the child who failed socially (the delinquent) than with the child who could not progress academically (learning difficulties). To the juvenile court case, the guidance clinic soon added to its caseload the children with more clearly defined of the neurotic and psychotic psychiatric symptoms; and these were eventually joined by their "character-disorder" peers!

During all those years, there were children with normal intelligence, fairly free of psychiatric symptoms and fairly well adjusted socially, who were not succeeding academically because of peculiar learning problems. Neurologists, psychologists, and educators showed concern for those pupils and studied extensively, each from his own viewpoint and usually in isolation, the phenomena that finally attracted the sustained attention of many child psychiatrists.

This new interest on the part of child psychiatry is not entirely spontaneous, for it results largely from the more recent tendency among the specialists referred to previously to seek the answer to these problems in a joint effort. This fairly new team approach to the learning difficulties of the child was bound to seek or attract the child psychiatrist; and although he feels a bit lost in this new field, he is showing more and more of a genuine interest.

In a child psychiatry service which is part of a general hospital, it is common to receive patients referred by the department of ophthalmology, neurology, or pediatrics, because of learning problems. For development and specialization of staff as well as efficacy of the service, the setting up of a learning problems clinic is appropriate. The usual team (psychiatrist, psychologist, social worker) is enlarged to include a neurologist and a specialized teacher.

Diagnostic and corrective methods in this particular area are far from refined and it is an extremely fertile ground for multidisciplinary research. Very few such clinics exist, at least in Canada; and these have met with such a strong response in medical as well as in school circles that it can be predicted that such clinics, within a child psychiatry service, will enjoy much popularity as far as case referrals are concerned and also will not lack financial assistance for research.

ADMINISTRATION STRUCTURE AND FUNCTIONS

In a pediatric hospital, the director of the child psychiatry service will usually be responsible to the director of the department of medicine, who in turn is responsible to the medical director and to the medical board, and through the latter maintains communication with the board of management of the hospital.

A large and very active child psychiatry service in a similar hospital, instead of being one of the several services of the department of medicine, could well be recognized as a full department and thus have the same administrative status as medicine, surgery, and laboratories. Such recognition may sometimes be necessary for the proper development of child psychiatry in a pediatric setting, because otherwise the needs of the child psychiatry service may not be fully appreciated and may be considered exaggerated by the hospital authorities when compared with the needs of such parallel services as dermatology and endocrinology.

In a general hospital, the child psychiatry service may administratively be part of either the department of psychiatry or the department of pediatrics. Aside from the administrative ties, it is obvious that the child psychiatry service requires a close relationship with the departments of psychiatry and pediatrics whose directors must lend strong support to the director of the child psychiatry service in relation to the Medical Board and the Board of Management.

A good deal of responsibility should be left to the director of the child psychiatry service in such areas as the selection of personnel and the preparation of budgets.

Within the Service

In terms of the clinical services, the staff of the child psychiatry service is grouped into specific entities which we have described as "clinics"—each clinic having its director-administrator.

There is also a staff grouping that takes into account each one of the several professions active in the service. These groups or "sections" are under the direction of the chief of the various disciplines: psychiatry, psychology, social service, nursing, nursery school education, remedial teaching, and administration (secretaries, typists, receptionists, etc.).

Meetings of the entire staff dealing with administrative problems should be held three or four times per year but their success will be conditioned by their preparation in smaller discussion groups consisting of the directors of clinics and the heads of sections. The director of the child psychiatry service should meet with the two latter groups of key people at least once a month.

STAFF

To function smoothly and effectively, the staff of a child psychiatry service must not only be competent in its own field but should also have special abilities to work as part of a team. To some extent, such a prerequisite is common to any type of psychiatric service but much more so in a facility for children where, so often, two or more members of a family are involved, whether in diagnosis or in treatment, with two or several members of the staff.

Such teamwork is fairly easy to achieve when the total staff is relatively small (i.e., 20 or less) but becomes a major problem with a larger staff, especially if the expansion of the service has been rapid. The multiplicity of personal idiosyncrasies added to the complex operation of scheduling team meetings constitute a chronic threat to genuine teamwork. It is important that it be a policy of the service to have each member of the staff prepare his work schedule during the preceding week, and to earmark three or four periods of time each week for such team meetings.

The scientific development of the staff should take place at various levels: (1) within each profession, through a weekly meeting of the various sections (psychology, social work, etc.), during which techniques of diagnosis, treatment, or reeducation proper to each discipline may be discussed around a case presentation or a theoretical seminar, and through the supervision and tutoring that the junior personnel receive from the more experienced staff in each profession; (2) within each clinic, the discussion of cases by participants of varied disciplines is mutually enriching but even more so are the regular meetings of such a team to reassess the overall quality of the clinic in terms of its own specific contribution to the service; (3) a weekly scientific meeting of the entire staff for clinical and didactic presentations, to which a prominent specialist is invited to lecture or to conduct the discussion on a case.

Partly because of the shortage of qualified specialists and consequently the sometimes fierce competition in recruitment, it is often deplored that the staff of a child psychiatry service is characterized by too much "mobility," not to say instability! Financial allurements are definitely not sufficient to ensure staff stability. The level of scientific life within the service, and the possibilities for research and teaching, the possibility of further training either inside the service or outside (for example, sabbatical year and summer sessions), the clear indication of gradual promotion to higher responsibilities, the leadership exercised in the service, and the general standing of the hospital, are all factors which for many valuable persons may well compensate for a less flamboyant salary.

Special problems arise regarding personnel practices when the service is part of a hospital: until recent years, there was a tendency for child psychiatric clinics operating under nonhospital auspices to offer its staff a more generous treatment than that offered by hospitals. In Canada at least, this discrepancy is expected to disappear soon, largely because of the influence of the government Hospital Insurance Service established in 1961. As a result of the financing of most hospital services by one central agency (the Provincial government), it has become clear that several paramedical professions essential to a child psychiatry service had not received adequate attention on the part of hospital administrations whose experience with nonmedical personnel had usually been limited to groups such as nurses and medical technicians. Furthermore, the government, now having a more direct responsibility in providing adequate services, realizes the importance of offering to such personnel conditions comparable to those common in private agencies.

An even more recent development is the formation of professional syndicates among hospital social workers, nurses, and teachers, which are affiliated with labor unions and use the legal privilege of collective bargaining with the employer. It is expected that the time is not too distant when the employer around the negotiation table will be the government representative.

The leveling of salary scales and the greater initiative of each profession are factors which will relieve the director of a child psychiatry service of time-consuming and difficult functions which he has had to perform, thus freeing him for professional activities for which he is better prepared.

It is of the utmost importance that each profession working within a child psychiatry service be informed clearly about the role it is expected to play in the service. For example, if the policy is to allow only a minor portion (20 percent) of the psychologist's time to psychotherapy of the children and the remainder is spent in diagnostic testing, this should be spelled out at the time a psychologist applies for a position. It would seem that such a restriction concerning the treatment of the children by nonmedical staff is wise, especially in a hospital structure; and, of course, such treatment should always be supervised regularly by a psychiatrist. Furthermore, those who show interest in undertaking therapy with children should be allowed to do so only after one year of duty in the service.

It is unrealistic to reject part-time staff and yet too large a proportion of such people on the staff often has a disorganizing effect. It appears that, in each profession, at least 50 percent of the staff should be on a full-time basis.

In our experience, a balanced proportion of staff for outpatient services is the following: one psychiatrist for two psychologists and two social workers.

In the inpatient clinic, the selection of the staff cannot be left entirely to the hospital nursing office; and in the last analysis, the psychiatrist in charge must decide on the right candidates. Those who are young, intelligent, kindly, warm-hearted, unsentimental, and with a good sense of humor are more likely to be successful. These qualities usually go with stability and a good relationship with their own parents in childhood and later. The uniform should not be too formal and hospital authorities must allow the nursing staff to take the children outside the grounds of the hospital for "therapeutic" outings or visits.

Recognition of the clinical aspects of some disturbed behavior in the child should not prevent a reasonable degree of kindly authority and the order that is essential to a child's security.

Visiting by relatives must have particular attention and can be utilized for therapeutic work with the home. Its regulations must vary according to each child's needs, much as does a medical prescription; the same applies to the child's visits to his home.

PATIENTS

The intake policy, with reference to the pathology of the child, has to be liberal if the child psychiatry service is part of a hospital, since it is traditional for a hospital service to accept, at least for an evaluation, any "sick" person. The maximum limit of age is usually 18, although the number of patients in the age group 15–18 will vary a good deal according to the interest in adolescent patients on the part of the local clinics for adults.

It is useful to have within the outpatient clinic some members of the various disciplines who take special interest in adolescents work more closely, thus forming a subclinic. Indeed, many aspects of the classic child guidance clinic approach to children and their parents do not apply to the adolescents and their parents; for example, frequency, duration, and content of the treatment session with the adolescent requires more flexibility than with younger patients.

Patients referred by the hospital naturally should take precedence over outside referrals: the latter should be examined in the pediatrics clinic before intake in the child psychiatry service unless they have been sent by private physicians or other hospitals.

In child psychiatry clinics, one finds a tendency to adjust the period of therapy with the academic year, which is probably the most significant "cycle" and time-orienting factor in the child's life. But such an approach is unfortunate when used for the treatment of an individual child, who, for instance, may require more therapeutic support during the summer months when he lives more intensively with his family. It is also unfortunate, in terms of the patients who did not have the chance of getting on the "caseload" of a therapist during September or October and thus must usually wait till the next fall!

The annual report (1962) of a large child psychiatry service shows that of a total of 1847 patients, 1107 were boys and 740 were girls. The breakdown according to age was the following:

0–5	yrs.	331
6–11	yrs.	1013
12–18	yrs.	503

In our experience, one basic outpatient team (1-2-2) can see approximately 300 new cases and provide sustained psychotherapeutic care (three to nine months) for approximately 50 children and their parents during a one-year period.

TEACHING AND TRAINING

In the training program of a child psychiatry service, priority should be given to the training of physician-residents in child psychiatry. Until 1957, when child psychiatry officially became a medical subspecialty, a large number of training programs in the United States were centered exclusively on outpatient clinics, usually child guidance clinics. The requirements of the American Board of Psychiatry have brought about close affiliation of such clinics with general or pediatric hospitals. A similar trend can be observed in Canada, where official recognition by the Royal College of Physicians of child psychiatry as a subspecialty was formally requested in 1963 by the Canadian Psychiatric Association.

The resident should come to child psychiatry after two years of training in general psychiatry. Whether or not he should have had a previous period of residency in pediatrics is debatable, but if he has not, his two-year program in child psychiatry should include at least six months of psychiatric training in a setting closely associated with a pediatric department or hospital.

The core of the clinical training should certainly be a prolonged experience (minimum of one year) in the closely supervised diagnosis and treatment of outpatients.

It has often been said in recent years that training programs for psychiatrists tend to overemphasize and idealize the role of the future psychiatrist as a private practitioner. The criticism is well founded, although it is obvious that other factors (psychological, sociological, and economic) contribute to this choice of private practice as the predominant avocation of so many psychiatrists.

Interest in other types of practice can be stimulated during residency by introducing into the program a variety of experience in areas such as institutions for the retarded, residential treatment centers, school services, juvenile courts public health services, and social agencies. Considering that many new child psychiatry services will have to be established in Canada in the next few years, it is also important that the resident be taught how to initiate and maintain such a service through theoretical and practical teaching in organization and administration.

Training centers in child psychiatry, as have been recommended by the Canadian Psychiatric Association, should be affiliated with a medical school. This is now a regulation of the Royal College of Physicians as far as general psychiatry is concerned.

The second most important teaching and training responsibility of a child psychiatry service is that of the medical (especially pediatric) and nursing staff of the hospital; and to this effect, the director of the child psychiatry service or a senior assistant should have a teaching appointment in the departments of pediatrics and of nursing. Full acceptance is necessary not only on the part of the pediatrician-in-chief but also of the chief resident in pediatrics.

Teaching to those two groups will be effective and appreciated if it is carried out in the natural habitat where these physicians work and with case material of their own. History-taking is a safe ground to use in teaching medical colleagues and here the child psychiatrist can share his skills with the pediatrician, in demonstrating his various interviewing techniques geared at eliciting all the facets of the child-parent relationship.

Pediatricians are also interested in learning how to handle the parents in their daily, busy practice and how to enlist their support in administering proper care to the child. They also expect us to help them devise psychological ways of preparing the child for medical or surgical procedures. The identification of early signs of psychopathology and the delineation between the disturbances that they should handle themselves and those for whom they should request a psychiatric consultation also constitute essential elements of our teaching to pediatricians.

Child psychiatrists must try to recapture vocabulary and ways of communicating which are specific to the medical profession as a whole and avoid speculations on the psychodynamics of a case unless it is based on symptoms or behavior which can readily be observed by the pediatrician. A psychiatrist whose nondirective approach is too deeply ingrained usually does not succeed very well in teaching nonpsychiatric colleagues whose natural tendency to expect "concrete" recommendations from a consultant or teacher would probably be frustrated by such a person.

The staff of a child psychiatry service should be utilized in hospital departments such as the prenatal clinic and the well-baby clinic. The staff should also be consulted when the hospital sets up policies concerning visits from the parents. One still sees too often pediatric wards where children whose physical condition does not require them to be bedridden spend long hours inactive, bored, and lonesome for lack of a proper daily program of academic, recreational, and therapeutic activities; and the child psychiatry service should offer suggestions to remedy such a situation.

The clinical teaching of child psychiatry to medical students should be integrated partly to the teaching of pediatrics and partly to the teaching of general psychiatry.

It is a responsibility of a child psychiatry service to offer training programs (internship, lectures, etc.) to students of all the disciplines represented on its clinical staff. Furthermore, this is obviously an excellent means of recruiting personnel and of creating within the service a high degree of scientific stimulation.

RESEARCH

A group of well-qualified professionals working in close liaison and eager to explore original techniques in the clinical services as well as in the teaching program are implicitly a research-minded staff. It has been our experience that in a service such as the one described here, the interest in research will become explicit and focused on specific areas of investigation only after the staff has concentrated, during several years, on rendering the patients and the hospital the best quality of clinical services. This is necessary not only to ensure a solid basis for future specialized research but also to prevent feelings of guilt in individuals who would choose to utilize part of their time in the service for research proper.

It seems that more meaningful research studies can be achieved by individuals who have grown with the service, so to speak, than by "importing" a research specialist whose task would be to develop and direct a research program. Among the several handicaps that such a person would face, one is the cool reception he might be subjected to by the staff, who often consider work in research as a privilege; and such a situation would stimulate conflicts of "class" or "caste" within the service.

In this respect, the traditional system of granting research money for specific projects presented by specific individuals, who then depend for their income on the yearly approval of the project, is not satisfactory. The budget of a service should allow the director to recruit personnel on the basis of their competence and the particular needs of the service, and it should have equal salary provisions, whether the individual will be mostly occupied with clinical work, teaching, or research. Not only does this provide financial security to research workers, but it also officially signifies that the administrative authorities (hospital, university, or government) recognize these three activities as equally important. It also tends to break down the artificial barrier between research and service which has to be erected, at least by administrators, when budgets are earmarked specifically for the former or the latter. Finally, such a flexible kind of budget allows the service to establish with better planning, the proper balance between services to patients, teaching, and research.

Some areas of research are particularly desirable for a child psychiatry service located in a children's or general hospital, such as prospective studies (in contrast to the more common retrospective ones) in collaboration with the prenatal and well-baby clinics and the obstetrics department; longitudinal studies, especially in psychosomatic disorders; psychological phenomena associated with growth and development for example, the so-called puberty and adolescence crisis as a cultural or inborn phenomenon in collaboration with pediatric endocrinology; the testing of psychoanalytic theories, such as castration anxiety with surgical patients; the study of the body-image concept in children in a traumatology department.

An up-to-date library is, of course, an essential element in any child psychiatry service that wishes to encourage the scientific

life of its staff. It should preferably be located on the premises of
the service and in the care of a full-time person, who should also
be available to staff members who wish to gather information and
material for the purpose of writing a scientific paper. Such a
person should preferably be a certified librarian and, if not, she
should at least be capable of being trained by the hospital librarian.

ANCILLARY SERVICES IN THE COMMUNITY

A child psychiatry service cannot fulfill its functions properly
without having a number of community resources at its disposal;
and since there are very few communities where all the needed
facilities are available, it becomes a duty for the child psychiatry
service to voice these needs to the various segments of society and
to advise public or private authorities on the organization of such
ancillary services.

A very large number of the patients in a child psychiatry service
cannot function in a regular classroom; that is, the educable and
semieducable retarded, the prepsychotic, the intelligent children
with severe learning problems, and some of the patients presenting
neurotic or personality disorders.

Other children may be able to cope with a standard school
situation but may present problems specifically related to and stimulated by the home environment. Here we enter into the vast and
unknown field of foster home placement. In view of the great
importance paid by the staff of a child psychiatry service to the
parents in terms of the diagnosis or treatment of a child, it is
puzzling to see that the same staff often devotes very little time to
assessing and working with the "new" parents once the child is
placed in a foster home.

Boarding institutions have undergone crises that affected their
very existence as a result of a voluminous literature on such topics
as maternal deprivation and hospitalism. Now that the emotional
components of this whole question of the separation from the
parents have abated, we see in sophisticated circles a gradual acceptance of the boarding facilities for certain children. The more recent

formula is the "group foster home," which certainly has much to offer the older child and the adolescent. Such a home could also be utilized by a child psychiatry service for children who may come from distant areas for a diagnostic evaluation. If it is located near the hospital, the child may spend the day in the inpatient unit or day clinic for observation and tests and reintegrate in the home in the evening. This is not only economical but often beneficial to a child overly threatened by hospitalization. The same type of group home can serve as a halfway house for children well enough to leave the inpatient clinic and yet not ready to reintegrate with the family.

Lastly, the child psychiatry service must have easy access to a children's psychiatric hospital where patients requiring long-term treatment can be referred. There are many advantages in setting up such a hospital of a small size (50 to 100 beds) near the pediatric or general hospital in which the child psychiatry clinic is located.

Community education is usually considered as being one of the responsibilities of a child psychiatry service. However, if one has in mind the community at large, there can be serious objections to being too active in that area, mainly because most child psychiatry services are already overwhelmed with requests for services and to attract directly or indirectly (often through education) new clients who cannot be served is certainly not a "healthy" gesture. However, education of specific, homogeneous groups, such as general practitioners, pediatricians, public health personnel, teachers, or social agency staff, can be extremely valuable, especially if it is geared to help such professional persons gain greater understanding of the child's behavior, and skill to handle minor cases which can thus be prevented from becoming major problems.

CONCLUSION

In Canada, the development of child psychiatry services within pediatric or general hospitals is a relatively new phenomenon, but we can already see the positive effects it has had on the community, the hospitals, medicine, and psychiatry. It has brought back child psychiatry into the mainstream of medicine and it has contributed to early case-finding and prompt therapeutic intervention.

The content of this paper is based on the author's seven years of experience in setting up a child psychiatry service at Ste-Justine's Hospital in Montreal, a large (760 beds) and modern pediatric institution for the French-speaking community. During the seven years, the staff grew from the original nucleus of 3 to the present group of 50 full-time professional persons, who gave their services to 2,500 children in 1963 as compared to 250 in 1957. The service consists of the six clinics described in this paper. The inpatient unit has 14 beds for boys under 13 and for girls up to 18 years of age and the day clinic is attended by 35 children who are brought daily by means of a transportation system organized by the service.

General and pediatric hospitals find it difficult to realize that psychiatry requires much more space for its clinical activities than most other specialties. Interview and treatment rooms, areas for the occupational, recreational, and pedagogic activities of the children attending the day clinic or the inpatient unit, group therapy rooms, an audio-visual laboratory, a conference room, and a library are all necessary facilities that need a great deal more space than the hospital had planned to allocate to a child psychiatry service, if it had planned any at all! Therefore, the building of a small pavilion adjoining the hospital and containing all the child psychiatric facilities may often be the answer to an almost insoluble problem.

In spite of its large staff, our child psychiatry service cannot adequately fulfill all the needs of the hospital; but then a children's hospital of such a size is unusual and in our opinion not to be recommended. The development of our service has now reached a plateau and the only sector which will continue to expand is the training of residents (their number could be increased from 6 to 12) so that some of the newly certified child psychiatrists, hopefully, will choose to leave the metropolitan area and organize services in other general hospitals of the Province.

This decentralization of the services is urgently needed in Canada and will only be possible if training programs attract at least twice as many candidates as they do now. In this respect, it is hoped that in the near future the Royal College of Physicians will establish child psychiatry as a bona fide subspecialty, since such a recognition would no doubt favor the recruiting and training of the additional 100 child psychiatrists necessary to meet the immediate needs of our country!

REFERENCES

1. American Psychiatric Association. *Psychiatric Inpatient Treatment of Children*. Washington, D.C.: The Association, 1957.
2. American Public Health Association. *Services for Children with Emotional Disturbances*. New York: The Association, 1961.
3. British Medical Association. *Report of Subcommittee on Child Psychiatric Services*. London, 1962.
4. British Ministry of Education. *Report of the Committee on Maladjusted Children*. London: Her Majesty's Stationery Office, 1955.
5. Buckle, D., and Lebovici, S. *Les Centres de Guidance Infantile*. Geneva: World Health Organization, 1958.
6. Canadian Department of National Health and Welfare. *Residential Treatment Services in Canada for Emotionally Disturbed Children*. Memorandum No. 5. Ottawa, April 1962.
7. Canadian Mental Health Association. *Mental Health Services: Special Services*. Report No. 4. Toronto, 1962.
8. Canadian Psychiatric Association. Brief Submitted to the Royal Commission on Health Services. Ottawa, May 1962.
9. Group for the Advancement of Psychiatry. *Contribution of Child Psychiatry to Pediatric Training and Teaching*. Report No. 21. New York, 1952.
10. Grunewald, K. R. Child psychiatry in Sweden. *Acta Paedopsychiat.* (Basel) 5:190-193, 1963.
11. Lapointe, J. B. Child psychiatry across Canada. *Canad. Psychiat. Ass. J.* 6:241-247, 1961.
12. Lazure, D. A child psychiatry service in a pediatric hospital. *Canad. Hosp.* 35:62-64, 1958.
13. Lazure, D., and Houde, L. *Proposed Standards for a Psychiatric Hospital or Service for Children*. Ottawa: Hospital Design Division, Department of Health and Welfare, 1963.
14. Scott, W. C. M. Child psychiatry in Great Britain. *Canad. Psychiat. Ass. J.* 3:120-131, 1958.

A Special Class Program
for the Rehabilitation of
Emotionally Disturbed Children

EDWARD   J.   ROSEN

In 1960, the author, for one-half day per week, joined the Special Education Department of an elementary school, with a student population of about 25,000, for the purpose of initiating a special class program for emotionally disturbed children. The department had gathered some 200 referrals showing severe academic problems with accompanying symptoms of emotional and behavioral disturbance.

It had been decided from the outset that the school would not enter into the field of psychotherapy and that the program would remain within the limits of educational methods and techniques, but that these would be modified by the insights afforded by psychological and psychiatric principles. We were of the opinion that the teachers could remain teachers and effectively bring about changes in attitudes, feelings, and personality without assuming the role of clinical psychotherapists. We anticipated that most of the children

The Special Class Program here described was a combined effort in which each member of the project played a significant and creditable part. It was initiated as a result of the vision of the Superintendent of the Etobicoke Elementary Schools, Dr. K. F. Prueter, and the Boards of Education of Etobicoke and of Metro Toronto. The team members included the Director of Special Education, Mr. J. Stinson; and the supervisors, Mrs. D. Izzard and Mr. R. Campsall; the school principal, Mr. D. Banks, and the author. The two teachers were Mrs. V. Marcus and Miss D. Barker.

and families chosen for this class would show extensive psychopathology, and that if psychotherapy were indicated the family would be sent to their own doctor for referral to a clinic or private psychiatrist.

Of the 200 cases mentioned above, 54 were selected as being most urgent by the school principal and the special education staff.

A detailed review of these 54 cases was carried out and this study included:

1. Complete school records
2. Individual intelligence tests
3. Statement of current problem by the teacher and principal
4. Interview with parents by teacher and principal
5. Public health nurse's report
6. Medical report from family doctor
7. Special medical reports, i.e., neurological or psychiatric consultations
8. Visits by members of the project team to the school to observe the child in the class, and to speak to the teacher, principal, and sometimes the parent

The 54 cases showed the expected preponderance of boys. There were 40 boys and 14 girls, 16 of these had been seen by a psychiatrist and several had been in treatment.

Recommendation and disposition of these 54 cases at the end of the first year were as follows:

Admitted to Thistletown Children's Hospital	1
Moved out of the township	3
Enrolled in private school	1
Over-age for proposed educational rehabilitation group, but needing constant guidance	4
Auxiliary or academic vocational class placement already made or planned for	4
Underage for special educational rehabilitation group	2
Withdrawn from school	2
Could be carried with reasonable success in regular classroom	

by combined efforts of our total staff, outside medical treatment and parent cooperation	21
Recommended for special educational rehabilitation group	16
Total	54

The conclusion reached by the study and presented in a recommendation to the Board of Education was that a special class program for 10 children under the age of 11 years should be set up as a pilot project. The class would have two full-time teachers and come under the supervision and guidance of the project team consisting of the director and supervisor of special education and the consulting psychiatrist. The two primary purposes of the class were:

1. To fully assess the learning and behavior problems of the child unable to function in the regular classroom.
2. To modify as much as possible the disturbed or disturbing behavior, and to raise the child to his best possible functioning level in order to return him to a regular class or other special classes with information that would be helpful in maintaining his steady progress.

Within two months of opening the class, it was clear to all of us that the program was producing good results more rapidly than we anticipated. The parent interviews confirmed our findings and also indicated that the change in behavior noted in the classroom had spread to the home and the community.

EXAMPLE OF TEACHER'S NOTES OF INTERVIEWS AFTER TWO MONTHS IN CLASS

Parent Interview

Extremely interested parents. Hardly through the door before they began to comment on the enormous change in Sandra. Very thrilled about the group and said that if Sandra was going to continue to change as she had done in the last few weeks, they hoped that we would keep her the rest of her school life.

Parent Interview

This was a very pleasant interview. They remarked immediately how very pleased they were with Mark's progress and of how changed they found him at home. They particularly stressed the fact that he was no longer afraid to talk to outsiders. They also remarked on his completely changed eating habits. Now they could never get enough for him to eat. They are very impressed with his reading. He now takes a book to bed every evening and will tackle almost anything. They said that his brother, David, accepts him much better now and they do many things together. They also remarked that he loves to play chess with his father. They are very pleased that he now plays hockey and other games with the boys.

CLASSROOM, TEACHERS, AND CLASS ROUTINE

The project was started in a small ten-room elementary school. The special class was called the "rehabilitation class" and became a part of the school under the authority of the principal, who played an important role in the project, becoming a member of the planning and supervisory team. The children of the rehabilitation class took the morning recess with the rest of the school, participated in the house league games, and attended the general assembly meetings. It was planned that when the child showed improvement, he would attend a regular class in the school for one or more periods. We intended to use this to test the child's progress and as a stepping-stone for him toward his return to a full-time regular class program in his own school.

We decided that the class of 10 children would best be served by two teachers. This would serve the following purposes: (1) allow a greater amount of time for a one-to-one teacher-pupil relationship; (2) make it possible for the class to continue its program while one or more children required special attention for disturbed behavior; (3) allow for continuity in the event of a teacher's absence; and (4) add the extra skills, initiative, resourcefulness, and beneficial effect of an additional well-trained, mature adult. Two teachers could increase each other's effectiveness and could support each other in the many unpredictable problems to be presented by the children in the day-to-day life of the class. Our faith in the two-teacher system was justified; and it is, we feel, one of the most important factors working toward the success of the project. The teachers chosen for the class had several years of teaching experience with normal and handicapped children. One had been on the staff of a children's psychiatric hospital, the other was an outstanding kindergarten teacher.

We were fortunate in our first venture to reap the rewards of an ideal team of teachers and encountered none of the problems that arise if the two teachers cannot work together with mutual respect and understanding.

The daily routine of the class was planned to include the following features:

1. A free activity period, tolerating a high level of noisy, active behavior
2. A quiet period for individual instruction and study
3. A gym period for special exercises and for free motor activity
4. Group projects, e.g., free discussion period, art, singing, and plays
5. Supervised lunch period

Observation and progress notes were kept by the teachers. The supervisors were available to the teachers for discussion and consultation from day to day. A full written report reviewing each child was discussed every three months and this was followed by a meeting with the parents.

THEORETICAL FRAMEWORK AND BASIS FOR METHODOLOGY

The clearest statement of personality development which underlies our method is the one presented by Erickson in his *Growth and Crisis of the Healthy Personality*. Using this scheme as a reference, we would expect that the healthy 6- to 10-year-old has developed a sense of trust in himself and in his world, as a result of the care, nurturing, and loving relationship with a mother and a father; that he has been allowed the freedom to develop his physical, psychological, and social potentials and thus acquired a sense of autonomy; that he has been free to explore the world about him, to express his own feelings, ideas, and fantasies, and thus developed a sense of initiative; and having accepted the challenge of the learning tasks presented by social relationships and the school curriculum, has attained a measure of a sense of accomplishment.

There are other features of his personality which are of critical importance, namely:

1. Impulse control and the ability to accept limits.
2. Reality testing, the ability to face and deal successfully with the demands of home, school, and community, and living without withdrawal into isolation, fantasy, or autism.
3. Responsiveness to adults and peer groups in meaningful and mutually satisfying relationships.
4. Satisfactory affect balance of love and hate, resolution of feelings of jealousy, anger, and frustration by socially acceptable behavioral patterns.

The ten children selected for the first special rehabilitation class showed disturbances in several or all of the areas of personality mentioned previously. The program and the methods used in this project are not unusual or novel in themselves. They are methods that could be used with great benefit in every regular class program.

DEVELOPING A SENSE OF TRUST
IN CLASSROOM

Basic and essential to the whole program were the establishment and maintenance of a strong feeling of trust. This we tried to do by the quality of the overall teacher-child relationship, reinforced for each child by the double experience with two teachers. The desired pupil-teacher relationship was that of mutual love. For those who find this word too strong we can substitute "mutual faith and respect." However, before we dilute the love relationship, either to avoid unacceptable sexual overtones or to keep ourselves in tune with the present-day cultural norm of superficiality in all relationships, let us examine the meaning of love as expressed by Eric Fromm in his *Art of Loving:* "Beyond the element of giving, the active character of love becomes evident in the fact that it always implies certain basic elements, common to all forms of love. These are *care, responsibility, respect,* and *knowledge.*"

The teacher gives the child an abundance of "care, responsibility, respect and knowledge," and in turn the child feels prepared to return some of the same to the teacher who has won his trust. The teachers give *care* by their individually planned program, by their presence in time of need, and by protecting the child from outer and inner forces which may threaten him. They show their *responsibility* by being explicit in all their dealings and instructions; by accounting for their actions; by a willingness to discuss any of the child's questions, comments, criticisms, or objections; and by attempting to understand his expressed and unexpressed needs. They respect his personal integrity both physically and psychologically. They maintain a ready *knowledge* of his feelings and his interests, and they remember all that he has revealed to them. The teacher's directness and openness at all times is essential in winning the child's trust.

The many opportunities for experiencing, developing, and testing a sense of trust in the teacher-child relationships arise from the close communication and interaction during individual tutoring sessions, collaboration when working on special projects, lunch period discussions, and spontaneous conversations throughout the day. The teachers must be mature and secure in their own personal adjustment and be given the freedom of action to create an atmosphere of acceptance in the class in their own unique manner.

In order to assure the development of this basic climate of trust, the supervisors must have faith and confidence in the teachers by allowing them freedom of action. No two teachers will develop the same climate in their relationship with a child, yet the effect may still be the same; namely, helping the child develop a sense of trust.

Example of Trust

John was an angry boy. He would sit at the table with his hands clenched, looking at the teacher and repeating, "You old bitch, I hate you, get away from me, I don't want to get your cooties." At first attempts to reach him in any way increased his anger, but after several months it was noted that his tone was less hostile and that he was becoming more involved in the class activities. Whereas the step of sending him home for misbehavior would not have been tried earlier, it was now judged that he could control his behavior. The next time he caused a disturbance he was sent home. The day at home made him conscious of the fact that he liked the class and the teachers, and that he trusted them. He began to bring some of his important possessions from home, asking the teachers to take care of them for him. He no longer berated them and wanted to sit or stand close to them all day. His academic work suddenly improved as did his relationships with the other children. He was "a changed boy." Trusting the children with material things was a meaningful way to give them evidence of a deeper trust in them. For example, Joe was allowed to take home a set of very valuable books belonging to one of the teachers. Eric was allowed to take the record player home. He was also allowed to paint one of the storage boxes and to use the carpentry tools in the classroom, neither of which was he permitted in his own home.

FOSTERING AUTONOMY
IN CLASSROOM

Most children feel that school imposes conformity and demands work with little concern for their individual needs. We know that the values and satisfactions of being a member of a social group require renouncing some of one's autonomy. Man's main evolutionary advances have come about as a result of his sociocultural achievements. In a society, individual autonomy is relinquished in return for the gratification possible in close interpersonal relationships and in the *"we-ness"* of belonging to a social group. The feeling of alienation of the "I-alone" is exchanged for the deeper and more meaningful "I-thou" and "I-we" relationships. In order to develop a true "I-thou" relationship, each individual must maintain a strong awareness of the "I" in himself, the "I" of a separate unique, worthwhile, autonomous being. Maintaining a sense of autonomy is a serious business for a child whose personality is unfolding and changing rapidly. Leaving the protection of his home, he will find the impersonal pressures of school a challenge to, if not an assault on, his sense of self-worth. If his low self-esteem is due to rejection at home, and he is resentful, hateful, and destructive, he will only bring about further rejection from the teacher and fellow students by being aggressive and disturbing in the classroom. For a child with this kind of problem the teacher's task is to find ways to show him that they respect his need for autonomy and respect his integrity and self-worth. In the class each child has his own books, desk, cubical, and time with the teachers. He may choose his own projects and write his own stories in his own way without correction. Every indication of self-expression is given recognition. He is not used or exploited, he counts for something in the group and is either protected from excessive harm or helped to combat threats to his personality by the use of his own strength and efforts.

DEVELOPING A SENSE OF INITIATIVE IN CLASSROOM

Some children are fortuntate during their developmental years in having the space, material, time, and freedom to express and develop their potentials on their own initiative. The space may be a garage, a basement, or a backyard; the materials wood, clay, string, wire, a motor, batteries, dolls, doll furniture, drawing material, a bird, a hamster, or a turtle. The time, a period of freedom, unencumbered by the need to produce something for somebody or for exhibition, and during which he may even choose to do nothing. Such a child must have the unusual combination of understanding and generous parents and a community in which living space has been allowed in its planning. Exploration on one's own initiative leads to wanting to know more and learn more about the world. The school system, according to modern educational principles, attempts to stimulate and aid the child to further his capacity to think clearly, critically, constructively and creatively, and to acquire work habits and study habits. However, the ordinary classroom does not seem to allow for full development of initiative. Some believe that the reason for this is that the classroom contains too many pupils in too small a space. One of our teachers places the blame fully on the choice made by the teacher, as an agent of a system that rewards her for reducing activity to a minimum, since a class that is sitting quietly and immobile, albeit cramped, suppressed, and dazed for five to six hours per day, is considered to be a well-behaved class under good control. Free and varied activities with the resulting minor or major personality conflicts can only be handled by a secure, capable, and well-trained teacher who can tolerate a moderate level of noisy interaction for some part of the day. Having children sit in a classroom, suppressing their need to communicate and to express their emotional and physical impulses, displays little consideration for the needs and benefits of the pupil himself.

In order to reawaken the sense of wonder and allow it to grow into a wish to learn as an answer to an inner need, the program of the rehabilitation class scheduled a free play period with a varied supply of materials and equipment. This period allowed the teacher and the supervisor to observe the child in individual activity and in his social relationships. It was then possible to explore ways in an active living situation to increase the child's ability to respond and to develop healthy patterns of behavior by encouragement, direction, or simply allowing him to develop these himself.

Example of Developing Initiative

Jim was very withdrawn. He just sat and watched others. He would do assignments but no more than asked and he never talked back. One day while he was watching the teacher hammering nails to make a pattern on wood, she turned to him and asked him to try. There was no response as usual. Next day he announced to her that he had thought it over and even dreamed about it and knew what he wanted to make. He was preoccupied with his plan for the next four days. He began to change in other ways. He questioned the amount of study work assigned to him. He resented being given directions. He showed anger and got into fights with the boys. The final evidence of change was that he laughed for the first time in his six months in the class.

Dorothy worked at two years below her level and was obviously afraid to try. One day the teacher remarked to her, "We don't mind if you make mistakes, we just want you to try," and on this day it seemed to reach her. She began to try and within a matter of weeks jumped about six months in her academic level. Sudden changes like this are not unusual in the children in this class; however, it is impossible to chronicle exactly for each child the experiences which have meaningfully accumulated to bring them to the point of sudden change. A host of experiences precludes the seemingly immediate reaction to a simple request for a change in attitude and performance.

DEVELOPING A SENSE OF ACCOMPLISHMENT IN CLASSROOM

Parents, teachers, and well-meaning friends and relatives will all agree as to the importance of trust, autonomy, and initiative once this has been fully explained, but no one has to be told about accomplishment. Stamped and written on every report card are the marks for tests and exams, yearly percentages, and the decision of promotion or failure into the next year. In our competitive society, children learn about success and failure long before they enter school.

A feeling of accomplishment is derived from having reached a set goal. But who sets the goal and how high will it be set? Will it be reached too easily or after a great deal of work and concentration? Or will it always and forever be beyond one's grasp? Parents set the goals by their demands and expectations. Some parents regard their children as infants; others expect them to have the control, concentration, knowledge, and understanding of young adults. The school curriculum is an inescapable testing ground and some children do not have the ability to keep up to the pace set by the curriculum. Some have been slow in maturing; and some have missed an important learning skill and may be floundering in confusion and failure for many months or years until they finally give up trying. It is obvious that the aim of the school program should be to allow the child to experience a sense of accomplishment in his classwork everyday and that this is the main function of the teacher and the school program. If the child falters, the teacher should be there to help him. If he fails, in spite of her help, this should be the signal of a problem of first magnitude. There are more reasons than one for failure of accomplishment and some may be stated briefly:

1. Maturational retardation
2. Social retardation
3. Child-teacher relationships causing anxiety
4. Child-parent relationships resulting in negativism, withdrawal, irritability, and motor restlessness
5. Poor teaching methods

Some children in their early school years show a cycle of being perfectly well during the summer months and a sudden onset of tension symptoms within the first week of school. The symptoms are carried on throughout the school term. These symptoms may be restlessness, sleep disturbances, enuresis, poor appetite, nail-biting, tics, or acting-out behavior disturbances. These are the children we were prepared to meet in the rehabilitation class. The children who feared, hated, and avoided school and had developed strong defenses against learning. In our program the teachers were prepared to allow the child to return to the beginning fundamentals of reading and arithmetic if necessary. They were aware that the child may not accept this temporary regression to the work of earlier grades since this only confirms his low self-esteem and feeling of failure and shame. More often, it was the parents who complained that their child was now working at a lower level than before. The teachers must somehow convey to each child that they have faith in his good potential and are ready to accept him for his good effort and success at any level. It may take weeks or even months to bring about this reorientation toward academic accomplishment. Once the child allows himself to be successful, he seemingly swells with pride in his new accomplishments. These successes at first belong to the close intimate world of a teacher-child relationship. We would not expect that his parents or his friends would comprehend his feelings upon grasping the fundamentals of numbers or of reading for interest and enjoyment.

Example of Accomplishment

It is difficult, if not impossible, to give separate examples for each, of trust, autonomy, initiative, and accomplishment, since they are so closely bound together. A child appears at times to take the full leap all at once, although there have been many weeks and many incidents that have gradually built up his inner strength to allow him to suddenly burst forth as a new person. For Stanley, age 12, simple division in arithmetic suddenly became clear to him and he wanted to show himself and others his new discovery again and again all day. His spontaneous expression of what it felt like to him was: "It feels just like Christmas."

ROLE OF THE PSYCHIATRIST

The psychiatrist's contributions as a member of the team in a project of this nature must be more than the obvious one of supplying an authoritative opinion about the presence, degree, and nature of psychiatric illness or emotional conflicts. Since the children have been or will be referred for medical consultation (including psychiatric), the psychiatrist will naturally act as the liaison member interpreting the school's position to the doctor and, in reverse, the medical findings to the school. The psychiatrist can make his most important contribution by offering adaptations of psychiatric principles which can be used in the class program. In so doing, the psychiatrist must remain aware of two facts: (1) that he is working within a well-established professional system with its own traditions and techniques; and (2) that the actual work with the children will be in the hands of teachers. Whatever modifications he may suggest must be easily assimilated by the team and have some chance of being brought into practice. The psychiatrist's main advantage is that he is in the favorable position of an knowledgeable outsider who is not bound by the limitations of the unquestioned assumptions and dogma that are part of the art and practice of education. Psychiatry has its own dogma and limitations, and hopefully one dogma (educational) is not merely being replaced by another (psychiatric). The goal of the psychiatrist is to help the educator free himself from his traditions in order to try new techniques. In recent years the educator has been deluged with many learning aids, usually involving some mechanical instrument which has the appeal of catching the fancy of the student. Most of these are mere gadgets and gimmicks. The use of individual tutoring aided by some learning device is merely an intensification, not a departure from, traditional methods. The innovation introduced in our project was that of "free activity," as used by children in their natural development and everyday learning. A simpler term for this is "play." However, play has come to mean the exact opposite of learning since there is some unfounded belief that "You can't learn while you play! You must work to learn!" Since school is considered a place to work and not to play, the use of play was at first questioned and mildly resisted by the project team, except for the two teachers, who had come to an independent decision about the use of the activity method and merely required the support of the psychiatrist. The use of play did unsettle some of the parents when their child reported every day that he enjoyed playing in the classroom. It took some time before the parents realized that their child's attitude toward school was changing for the better. Since the children began to show improvement in their academic work within a few months, the program could not be dismissed with doubt and misbelief. We have had children who required more than a year before they showed change. Fortunately, our first 10 children were not all of this order.

In the rehabilitation class, play allowed the child to explore a wide range of the objective world, to express his wishes, to release his emotions, and to enter into new relationship patterns with other children and adults. Play was also used as a reward: unless the assigned studies were completed, as much of the play period as necessary had to be used by the child to complete his work. Having to complete an assignment while others were back to their play activities was a strong incentive to finish quickly, and this they did at a speed that astonished even themselves. Of course, everything was not this simple: children who feel deprived are negativistic and fearful of even trying; and they require maneuvering, manipulation, confrontation, encouragement and restraint. This is more than can be wrapped up in a simple program of contrasting periods of play and study. The task of two teachers was to use every opportunity offered by individual or group behavior to facilitate and enhance either healthy expressiveness or reasonable control.

SETTING LIMITS AND CONTROLS

The children were informed upon entering the class that they would be expected to conform to certain rules and regulations. These were explained as reasonably as possible and it was established early that they would be put into force when necessary. Some of these were: (1) the time limits for each period, (2) the rules of behavior in the corridors and the schoolyard, and (3) the degree of disturbed behavior which would be allowed in the classroom and in the taxi coming and going to school. If the child lost control in the classroom he was removed to the nurse's room for a time. If it appeared as if he would not be able to regain control he was sent home for the day.

The learning and therapeutic implications of being removed from class or being sent home were: (1) a clear and definite expectation was set for the child; (2) the child was confronted with his problems or conflict; (3) the parents were confronted by the fact that there was a problem; (4) the child became aware of his positive feelings regarding his social needs; (5) the child became aware of his negative or positive feelings about the teachers; and (6) the child became aware of a strength for control outside of himself.

It was necessary to use some flexibility with respect to the expectations placed upon each child, and these were increased as it was felt that the child could handle them. There was "freedom within limits" and "expectations to the full potential for success."

THE GROUP AS
A THERAPEUTIC FORCE

Parents hesitate to place their child in a special class for the same reasons that they avoid admission to a psychiatric hospital. They don't want to think of him as being different from the norm. They don't want him labelled as a problem and thus have to face the true nature of his difference or illness. The child may share the parents' feelings about being separated from the normal stream, but it is surprising how quickly he becomes aware of the positive values of his new situation in the special class. Whereas in his previous situation he was isolated, friendless, and could not be helped or use the help offered, he suddenly finds himself in a group that exists expressly for his benefit. He is not alone. There are others like himself and he loses his feeling of being different. He cannot escape the conclusion that the program is being arranged for him and his group, and that someone, if not the many persons involved, deems him worthwhile. He finds that he is wanted and expected to become a participating member of a small ingroup, and this awakes, stimulates, and satisfies his normal social needs.

Jonathan's case is a good example of group influence. Jonathan was a lonely, isolated child in his own school. He had no friends and would hang about the school after hours to peer into the windows at his teacher or lie hiding in the ditch waiting to catch a glimpse of her when she left in the late afternoon. In the rehabilitation class, Jonathan was soon relegated to his usual role as scapegoat and was abused by the children. They identified his remoteness and lack of identity by calling him "false-face." A change came about when some children from the other classes began to push him at recess. The children in the rehabilitation class, both the boys and the girls, came to his aid. They identified him as one of themselves; they fought for him and encouraged him to stand up for himself. This incident helped the group become aware of their kinship feelings, and it helped Jonathan to gain an awareness of a sense of belonging and self-worth. His masklike face gradually relaxed and was replaced by a genuine smile. He would look at the person to whom he was speaking; and at times he exercised his new self-assuredness to the point of being cocky and belligerent.

The program was arranged to allow for a great deal of freedom in order to achieve a high degree of interaction among the children. The learning child has a vast capacity and need for trial and error experiences with much repetition. Since nothing is as complex as human interaction, the opportunity for exercising social skills again and again is essential to the developing child. A quiet and immobile class of children all looking in one direction, speaking only to the teacher and being answered only by her for six hours each day is the very antithesis of an opportunity to learn to live in a group. In the ordinary class the teacher exhausts herself in her daily struggle against the natural need for group interaction as she tries forceably to efface all lines of communication, other than those directed to herself. Such a teacher must feel as though she were continuously trying to sweep back the tides all day. In the rehabilitation class, except during the quiet study period or the discussion period, the children were free to mingle and interact according to their needs and wishes. The words of a kindergarten child who came home to report to her mother about school are examples of how children feel about the regular class system: "I can't read, I can't write and now I can't talk. They don't let you think—they say get on with your work."

An invitation to the group to participate in the school Christmas program offered both an opportunity and a challenge. They wanted to show that they were not "a dumb class" or a "peculiar class." They put a great deal of effort into making their costumes and learning their lines. Group pride and morale rose to an all-time high when they were told by the other children that they had presented the best play in the program. For one girl in the class, the experience marked a turning point in her progress. From September to December she was a passive, unexpressive, and excessively dependent child. She worked well on some occasions but most of the time she would sit and stare at a page for 20 minutes. On the playground she would stand on the fringe of the group just watching the games. The group with its innate perceptiveness had nicknamed her "fish-face." The enthusiastically appreciative audience gave her a feeling of accomplishment; and as she walked off the stage, her face glowed with delight. Her new animation and quiet happiness continued to increase from that time. She became the first child to spend part-time in a regular class and was returned to her home school at the beginning of the next school year. She continued to maintain her new level of functioning 1½ years later.

REVIEW OF FIRST TEN CHILDREN
ADMITTED SEPTEMBER 1961

1. Girl, age nine years, four months: I.Q. of 103, achievement was poor. She rarely completed any work, day-dreamed, was timid, conforming, friendless, fearful, and shy of adults. Preoccupied with death and accidents, she was under psychiatric treatment prior to admission to the class and this was terminated in December 1961.

A dramatic change in personality functioning began in January 1962. She became alert, outgoing, friendly, completed academic assignments, and soon was up to her grade level. She was returned to her regular class in September 1962 and in follow-up in September 1963 was reported as doing average work, participating in the classroom and on the playground.

2. Girl, age nine years, eleven months: I.Q. of 104, achievement poor, day-dreaming, bossy, doesn't care, difficult to manage, demands a great deal of attention.

She was in the class for 1½ years until April 1963. There was some improvement but the reason for returning her to regular class was that she had outgrown the class. In the follow-up in September 1963, she was reported as happy, friendly, and completing her work (aided by a very capable classroom teacher).

3. Girl, age nine years, one month: I.Q. of 116, achievement was borderline. She was unhappy, annoying other children and preventing them from learning.

In the rehabilitation class she varied in her productivity due to frequent moody periods. She could be happy and concentrate well for a time and then change to depression and irritability. The home situation was considered as the disturbing factor and the family were referred to a psychiatric clinic where progress was poor. We recommended boarding school but this was not followed out. She was returned to a regular class in September 1962, having improved academically and having managed to keep friendly relationships with her age group.

Follow-up in September 1963 found that she had spent a very successful year in the regular class, both academically and socially. The teacher's report was "likable girl with a difficult home life."

4. Boy, age nine years: I.Q. of 89, achievement low, untidy, inattentive, withdrawn, talks to himself, no friends, difficult to reach, escaping more and more from reality into fantasy. He was seen at the psychiatric clinic, diagnosed as seriously disturbed, and in-patient treatment was recommended (borderline schizophrenia).

Report, 1962: December 1962, I.Q. 104, improved in every respect. Report, 1963: Returned to regular class in February of 1963. Principal noted a marked change, since previously it was like talking to someone who wasn't there. He was joining in the class activities, smiling, responding, and spontaneously offering comments. Socially he was in one of the play groups in the schoolyard. He was one of the children most helped by the project.

5. Boy, age nine years, ten months: I.Q. 92. Report, 1961: He repeated grades one and two. Reading disability; little comprehension in arithmetic; much morbidity, hostility, and fear; loses control quickly.

Report, September 1963: Great improvement in all subjects. Takes pride in his work, enthusiastic. He progressed from end of grade one to grade four level in two years. Returned to regular grade with recommendation that he go to vocational school the following year.

6. Boy, age ten years: I.Q. 100, was in grade two for three years, achievement poor, slides out of responsibility, immature, over-active.

There was a marked improvement in social and work habits and he was returned to a regular class in September 1962 because it was felt that he required one year there before entering a vocational school. A follow-up in September 1963 found that he had a good year in regular class and was coping with the new program in vocational school.

7. Girl, age seven years: I.Q. 60 (tentative). Defiant, attacks other children, tantrums, hyperactive. Psychiatrist recommended residential or institutional setting but parents refused to follow advice. Marked maternal rejection.

In the rehabilitation class, she could not be handled other than with individual attention. She was hyperactive, with explosive emotional outbursts, annoying and fighting with the other children. Since she kept the class in a constant turmoil, she had to be excluded and placed on home instruction.

8. Boy, age nine years: I.Q. 93. Disrupts class with antics, pushing, fighting in playground, stoning girls, and is impudent and insolent. Rejected by parents. Completely lacking in self-worth.

Seen about once a month at psychiatric clinic. On several occasions it was thought that he would require hospital treatment. There was a long and unbroken period of the same disturbed behavior. Some evidence of change began to appear in January 1963, and in the spring he was returned to a regular class. In October 1963, he was reported as having adjusted quickly to his new surroundings and was a sport's monitor. Academically doing average work, the principal found him a changed boy.

9. Boy, age ten years: I.Q. 85 (tentative). He repeated grade three, is lethargic, has little self-discipline, sits doing nothing all day, and hates reading. He was seen twice at psychiatric clinic, not treated.

He made slow but steady progress and was returned to a regular class in September 1963. In the regular class he was described as a friendly, cooperative boy, a slow worker but good in arithmetic, had little trouble making friends, eager competitor in interschool sports.

10. Girl, age seven years, repeated kindergarten, no number sense, pencil work a scribble, was passive, remote, and was diagnosed as emotional disturbance with autism.

In our class she showed some progress in attentiveness and ability to relate. She was returned to a class for slow learners in September 1962. In September 1963 she was reported as quiet, but not withdrawn, works diligently and enters freely into all activities, progress slow, reasoning power poor.

SUMMARY

Twenty-three children have been admitted to the rehabilitation class from September 1961 to October 1963. Eleven of these children have been returned to the school program much improved and making good progress; one was returned to kindergarten after two months in the class because the problem was one of delayed maturation; and one was excluded after three months. The other ten have been in the class for two months to one and one-half years and are in various stages of improvement but insufficient to warrant returning to the school program. In September 1963, a second class was opened for ten children in the age range of seven to nine years. The original class was reserved for an older age group of nine to eleven years.

There were several benefits over and above the improvement in the children that must be mentioned as important features of the program:

1. Although the work with the parents was limited to a few interviews with the teachers and occasional discussion with the principal and supervisors, many of the parents gained a better understanding of the nature of the child's problem and were able to make changes in their own attitude toward their child. We

would have preferred to have had regular casework with the parents but this was not possible.

2. The classrooms from which our children had come were no longer being distracted and disturbed by them, leaving the teacher free to devote more time to the business of teaching some 30 other children.

3. Consultations with the school principals during our first survey and as part of the continuing service resulted in many children being handled with success in the regular school program, hopefully preventing their condition from reaching the stage that would require our special class placement.

4. Some children in the rehabilitation class made great strides without psychiatric treatment, while in others the class and the treatment augmented each other.

5. Immeasurable, but hopefully widespread, were the effects of this program within the school system. The case conferences were a learning experience for the special education department and its staff of school assessment officers who examine hundreds of children every year referred by principals for a variety of problems. It was a learning experience for the principals and teachers, since each case was discussed both before and during the class placement. In visiting the school it was possible to point out the need for earlier recognition of problem behavior so that remedial measures could be taken to prevent the development of more serious problems. The principals and the teachers who had been battling it alone were relieved by having a clear statement about the extent of the problem with which they had to deal, although all of the children could not be removed to a special class. The success of the program is attested to by the fact that it continues to have the full support of the school principals, who are the final judges of the practical value of the program to the school.

The Learning Center

M . SAM RABINOVITCH

The Learning Center was formally established at The Montreal Children's Hospital, a general pediatric hospital, in June of 1960. It was launched as a result of the common concern of psychiatrists, psychologists, and pediatricians, with children who were unable to learn in a manner and at a rate expected of them: children who had great difficulty learning, particularly but not exclusively, in the formal school setting; children who were not mentally deficient and not primarily psychiatric problems in the traditional sense, but who were, nevertheless, chronically frustrated in learning situations and quickly developing secondary motivational and attitudinal problems which were acting to undermine further their learning ability. The greatest number of children have come to the center because of their inability to learn to read adequately. A number have come because they were so "disorganized" as to be unable to cope with the school regime. Many of the younger children have come because their nursery school teachers felt that, while they were intelligent, they were not ready for formal schooling. This usually meant poor physical coordination, very short attention span, distractible, and excessive restlessness. Very often these children, young and old alike, seem to fit the category of what many writers have called "minimally brain injured."

Referrals to the center have come from schools, physicians, and parents. The patients have ranged in age from 4 to 17 years. They have all continued their regular school program while attending the

205

center. Frequency of coming to the center will to a large extent
depend upon the needs of each patient. The majority come twice
weekly for a total of three hours; many come more frequently; and
none of the children come less frequently. The usual pattern is for
a child to begin working alone with a teacher and, if it seems
indicated, to work eventually in a group of two or possibly three.

The center is staffed by a director (presently a psychologist),
five remedial teachers, two psychologists, and a psychiatrist. The
functions of the center can be grouped under three general headings:
service, training, and research.

SERVICE

The program of the Learning Center revolves around its service
function. Each youngster referred to the center is evaluated by one
of the psychologists and, as indicated, by the psychiatrist. The
youngster is evaluated by the usual psychological and educational
tests and, in addition, by a series of diagnostic devices which we
have taken or adapted from Kephart (2), Strauss and Lehtinen (3),
Strauss and Kephart (4), Zazzo (6), Benton (1), and Taylor (5).
These diagnostic techniques help to chart a variety of abilities and
help us discover relevant deficits. We have found it particularly
useful to evaluate the ability to appreciate spatial relations and
to function in situations demanding knowledge of such relationships. Similarly, it has been helpful to evaluate body image, knowledge of left and right, degree of lateralization of functions, and
the ability to appreciate and to produce rhythm. We study carefully
the degree of organization of temporal ability, the child's ability to
order events, or elements, into meaningful sequences, and his ability
to deal with form, color, and direction. When we know something
of the youngster's cognitive structure, we try to relate this knowledge
to his learning deficit, and often to his social and personal difficulties.
It is surprising how often an extremely poor writer demonstrates inadequate or erroneous finger localization, and how often he is
helped by playing with finger puppets. How often the poor speller

cannot cope with problems which require sequencing of events or objects, and how often he is helped by carefully graded play-like activities which gradually encourage him to cope with order at increasingly complex levels.

Above all, the diagnostic evaluation is aimed at charting a remedial course for each youngster. This invariably means that one must make explicit not only his deficits but also, more important, one must discover the conditions under which learning is achieved. It seems to be extremely helpful to know how to alter conditions so that some degree of success is possible, and using that as a baseline to proceed with further learning. With this in mind, it has often been interesting as well as useful to categorize youngsters according to sensory modes. Many of the diagnostic tests can be presented as visual and auditory, and some as tactual. Responses can be visually dominant, verbally dominant, or kinesthetically dominant. By presenting the tests in various ways, it sometimes becomes clear that a particular child learns much better through visual modes than any other way; or that auditory modes are his forte; or that without significant kinesthetic involvement, his learning is poor. Such observations make it easier to plan successful training activities.

It must be remembered that throughout the assessment and the subsequent training periods, the staff of the Learning Center have easy access to consultations with pediatricians, neurologists, electro-encephalographers, opthalmologists, otolaryngologists, speech therapists, audiologists, physiotherapists, and occupational therapists.

There is another very important aspect of the service role played by the center. This concerns the liaison between home and center, and between school and center. Parents are often encouraged to be present during the entire diagnostic procedure so that they can begin to understand more about their child's difficulty. When the diagnostic evaluation is completed, a concerted effort is made to interpret all of the findings to the parents, and each parent is immediately enlisted as an active participant in the therapeutic program. Following this, the child's teacher will act as the liaison between center and home, listening to parents, making suggestions to them, and trying to cope with their anxieties and their questions. Here again, each teacher is free to consult with anyone, especially the psychiatrist.

The liaison between the center and the school is carried out by a highly skilled and experienced teacher who is seconded to the center by the local school authorities. After having spent several months in the center working with children, reading, and attending conferences, this teacher begins the job of interpreting the center's program to school principals and teachers. Her contacts are centered around specific cases. The principal and teacher of each child in the Learning Center will be visited. In addition, principals are free to request a visit from the liaison teacher to discuss any specific children they wish to help. Our experience has been that this type of liaison work is invaluable. It appears to be a rather powerful agent in modifying attitudes of educators about children with learning problems.

TRAINING

School authorities, mental health clinics, and nursery schools from several cities have used the Learning Center as a training resource. Psychiatric residents training in child psychiatry regularly participate in the program, as do psychologists in training.

RESEARCH

There has been from the start, and continues to be, considerable conviction that our greatest need is for more knowledge about the cognitive organization of these children with learning difficulties. We have tried to integrate our research activities with the overall program of the center.

When the center was established, certain basic notions were established to serve as a broad theoretical framework. It was assumed that learning is a function of the central nervous system. The brain serves to receive, organize, and store experience, and these functions of the central nervous system determine behavior. The brain is, in fact, shielded from the environment and from the rest of the organism and must rely on the exteroceptive, interoceptive, and proprioceptive senses to feed in the information to be organized and stored. It follows that one must pay considerable attention to the various senses and how they function. But it is essential that one never lose sight of the fact that the senses are only a means to an end.

Logically, the child's concept of his body—its capabilities, its limitations, and its topography—seemed of singular importance. As well as making theoretical sense, the body-image notion also seems important from an empirical point of view. Many of the children with learning problems seem to have rather peculiar notions of their body, and many of them seem to be extremely inept at manipulating various parts of their body. Thus, Allan at age six was unable to use a pair of scissors. After one week of daily home activities in which Allan's attention was drawn to his individual fingers (e.g., they were named, they were used in several finger games, they were used in finger puppets), Allen was again handed a pair of scissors and this time had no particular trouble in setting his fingers properly and using the scissors. The question of muscular coordination comes to mind. It hardly seems likely that one week of training could have overcome a deficit in muscular control. It seems much more probable that the training activities provided the sensory information which enabled Allan to consolidate a more adequate central image of his hand. In any case, this is the type of experience which has aroused our interest in the notion of the body image. Looking into the literature, we found that there was much speculation but little reliable data about the normal development of body image. There is data from the field of neuropathology clearly establishing a connection between body-image deficits and specific brain lesions, particularly in the parietal lobe. There is the interesting work on the phantom limb phenomena with the emphasis on proprioceptive input as the basis of body-image development.

Starting with the work recently reported by Benton (1), we have done some finger localization studies on children beginning at age four years and going up to age nine. Data have also been collected on blind children, in an effort to isolate the possible role of visual experience in developing an image of the hand. The evidence at this point tends very much to support the notion that while proprioceptive input is crucial in developing an image of the hand, there is likely a visual spatial component which is measurable because under certain conditions it interferes with performance. We have also worked out a simple way of measuring body-image knowledge for many other body parts and this method clearly shows up our Learning Center patients to be grossly deficient. It may be of interest that when we tested certain types of subjects, namely track and field stars and ballet dancers, they demonstrated rather superior performance in the body-image measurement situation.

As we worked with the children in the center, several other aspects of their behavior seemed to warrant investigation. Many of them were "arhythmic;" that is, they seemed to be unable to walk, talk, or work in rhythmic fashion. Data were collected on normal children in a rhythm tapping test and again it was found that the Learning Center children were inferior to the normal children in this task.

Another study may be of interest here, particularly because it may be related in some way to the problem of rhythm. The experiment is one in which different number series are simultaneously presented to each ear. In normal subjects, both adults and children, when the numbers are presented at one-half second intervals, the usual response is to *first* report the series that was presented to the preferred ear, and then report the series that was presented to the other ear. This suggests that the subject stores up one side while he reports the other. The Learning Center children try to do this but are much less efficient than the normals; they make many more errors. If the time interval between presented pairs of numbers is increased to one and one-half or two seconds, the normal subjects change their mode of reporting. Instead of reporting one ear and then the other, they now systematically go back and forth and report what has been called a "temporal order" rather than an "ear order." It has been argued that the subject in the original experiment has to respond automatically because the numbers come so quickly. However, in the situation with the longer time interval, the subject "rehearses" the numbers and "reorganizes" the series into the "temporal order." We found that the children with learning problems could not manage this reorganizing behavior. They became confused and would desperately hold onto the "ear order" mode of response even though they were performing inefficiently.

Another study concerned the problem of sequential behavior, or serial order, using a group of little tests designed to measure the child's ability to order events. In a normal population, children from age 3½ to 12 years clearly demonstrated that as age increases, the ability to order events improves. Children with learning problems did rather poorly when compared with the normals. They seemed to have trouble organizing the situation when the task required them to respond in definite sequences as, for example, in the Knox cube test, where four blocks are mounted on a piece of wood, and the experimenter touches one block after another according to prearranged sequences. In this situation, the Learning Center subjects were able to reproduce the correct number of touches but not the correct order of touches.

These are examples of the research activities in the center. As cognitive deviations are observed in training activities, we have tried to investigate them. At this stage the main effort is to define as clearly as possible the nature and extent of these deficits in order to plan more adequate training activities, and in order to develop eventually a comprehensive, reliable system for evaluating children with learning problems.

In summary, it may be said that the Learning Center is an "ego psychology center." This is the theme of the program: an attempt to learn how to do more in the way of providing ego skills to youngsters who have, for whatever reasons, not managed to develop these skills on their own.

REFERENCES
1. Benton, Arthur L., *Right-Left Discrimination and Finger Localization: Development and Pathology.* New York: Paul B. Hoeber, 1959.

2. Kephart, Newell C., *The Slow Learner in the Classroom*. Columbus: Charles E. Merrill, 1960.
3. Strauss, Alfred A., and Lehtinen, Laura E., *Psychopathology and Education of the Brain-Injured Child*. New York: Grune and Stratton, 1947.
4. Strauss, Alfred A., and Kephart, Newell C., *Psychopathology and Education of the Brain-Injured Child. Progress in Theory and Clinic* (vol. 2). Grune and Stratton, 1955.
5. Taylor, Edith Meyer, *Psychological Appraisal of Children with Cerebral Defects*. Cambridge: Harvard University Press, 1961.
6. Zazzo, René, *Manuel pour L'Examen Psychologique de L'Enfant*. Neuchâtel (Switzerland): Delachaux and Niestlé, 1960.

Index